Echoes from Old China

夏威夷華人歷史研究中心出版

中國古代風俗文化

西醫博士婦產專科譚金成著

Echoes from Old China

LIFE, LEGENDS AND LORE
OF THE MIDDLE KINGDOM

K. S. Tom, M.D.

Hawaii Chinese History Center • Honolulu

First printing 1989
Second printing 1990

This book is printed on acid-free paper and meets
the guidelines for permanence and durability of
the Council on Library Resources.

Library of Congress Cataloging-in-Publication Data

Tom, K. S., 1915–
Echoes from old China: life, legends, and lore of
the Middle Kingdom / K. S. Tom.
   p. cm.
   Includes bibliographical references.
   ISBN 0-8248-1285-9
   1. China—Social life and customs. I. Title.
DS721.T59 1989
951—dc20   89-20224
                   CIP

Distributed by
University of Hawaii Press
2840 Kolowalu Street
Honolulu, Hawaii 96822

To the Memory of

My Parents
Mr. and Mrs. Tom Young
先父譚養　先母譚歐妙顏

and

My Wife's Parents
Mr. and Mrs. Chun Hoon
先岳父陳寬　先岳母陳李愛

CONTENTS

0 200 400 600 800 1000 km

Kun Lun Mountains

SINKIANG

KANSU

Khotan

CHING HAI

TIBET

INNER MONGOLIA

HEILUNGKIANG

KIRIN

LIAONING

KOREA

Peking

Tientsin

Yellow River (Huang Ho)

HOPEH

SHANSI

SHANTUNG

Yellow River

KIANGSU

SHENSI

Kaifeng

Loyang

Sian

HONAN

ANHUI

Nanking

Shanghai

HUPEH

Hankow

Hangchow

CHEKIANG

SZECHUAN

Yangtze River

Chungking

HUNAN

KIANGSI

FUKIEN

TAIWAN

KWEICHOU

West River

(Hsi Kiang)

KWANGTUNG

YUNNAN

KWANGSI

Macao

Canton

Hong Kong

HAINAN

PREFACE

In old China, the Ching 清 dynasty (1644–1911) began as a period of brilliant achievement. For over a century, skillful administration and judicious control kept peace throughout the empire. Relations with the border states were good, and learning and scholarship flourished. But by the beginning of the nineteenth century, the dynasty of great splendor was deteriorating rapidly. Internal decay and intrusions by foreign powers were the ominous signs of an empire in distress. Government officials became increasingly incompetent and corrupt, and revolts broke out on a wide scale. Political unrest, banditry and peasant uprisings seemed to be the order of the day.

As if that were not enough, droughts and floods caused widespread famine. Trade in opium, forbidden by the emperor, mounted rapidly. For the peasants of China, about four-fifths of the population, there seemed to be little prospect of escaping the abject poverty that extended in all directions. Many concluded that their only hope was to leave their homeland.

The first emigrants from China were mainly from the two southern provinces on the Pacific Ocean, Fukien 福建 and Kwangtung 廣東. These emigrants journeyed to many parts of the world. They took with them their culture, customs and traditions, and transmitted their understanding of life to their children and to their children's children. As a result, something of Chinese history and culture has survived and been preserved in foreign lands. Yet, as might be expected, some old customs were modified, forgotten or even deliberately discarded. And when the young asked, as they always do, why things had to be done in a certain way, the elders often did not know the answer. They had to brush the inquiries aside by saying it was for "good luck."

Today the Chinese living abroad, particularly the young adults, have found a renewed sense of pride in their race and its accomplishments. They are naturally inquisitive about their roots and their heritage. The emergence and opening of the new China have stimulated a keen and intense interest in the original homeland. For readers such as these, as well as for non-Chinese who may be curious about China and things Chinese, this book provides a general introduction to Chinese customs, traditions and culture. It is by no means an exhaustive or definitive account of the topics that have been selected for discussion.

The material in this book represents a distillation of my personal experiences and things that my parents, grandparents and other elders with special knowledge or lore have shared with me. Also included are things I have learned in Chinese language school and in my own study of written sources. The customs and traditions I describe are mainly those that were practiced more than a century ago in southern China—and specifically, in the village of Ko Tien 隔田 near the town of Shih Chih 石岐, the capital of Chungshan 中山 district in Kwangtung province. This area, adjacent to Macao 澳門, was the home of my ancestors.

Some may disagree with certain things in this book. It must be noted that China is a large country—one-third larger than the United States, excluding Alaska and Hawaii. It encompasses a tremendous variety of different ethnic and language groups. Chinese terms for the same object differ according to what part of the country the speaker is from. Even within the same area, customs often varied from village to village. In our family, whenever there was a difference of opinion regarding how certain traditions should be observed, my parents consulted our older paternal aunt. If she said, "This is how we did it in our ancestral village," we followed her advice. If she did not know the answer, she dismissed it by saying, "It does not matter if it is half-Chinese and half-foreign, it will be all right."

It is my hope that this book will serve as a basic primer, providing a new understanding of things Chinese. If the reader's interest is kindled and additional information is desired, there are many books in English that offer further details. A representative list of such texts is provided in the bibliography.

ACKNOWLEDGMENTS

It is impossible to acknowledge individually all of my friends who contributed information which I included in this book. Many did not realize that they had provided me with interesting facts. Nevertheless, credit must be given to Nellie and Minto Loo, Neuman Pei, Hing Leong Lau, Francis and Lily Chong, Cecilia Lo, Peggy Eu, Dr. Eugene N. Wong, Mabel Chang, Thelma Zen, Wing-Tat Lee, Harry Ho and Albert Chun.

The families of my brothers and sisters, my sons, my wife's brothers and sisters and some of their children were most generous in providing financial support for the publication of this book. I am deeply grateful to James and Mary Nip, Francis and Lily Chong, Kam Hin and Johanna Tom, Warren and Gladys Chun, Robert and Helen Yee, William and the late Mabel Wong, William and Susan Tom, Joseph and Mabel Tom; Dr. Lawrence and Mary Tom, Dr. Douglas and Marilyn Tom, Allen and Rita Tom, Dr. Curtis Tom; the Chun-Hoon Trust, Kam Quon Chong, Helen Chun-Hoon, Edith Chun-Hoon, David and Marion Mar, Judge Chuck and Karen Mau, Kenneth and Alice Chun-Hoon, Hal Yee, Dr. Arthur and Peggy Chun-Hoon, Robert and Mabel Chang, Thelma Zen, Dr. William and Marjorie Chun-Hoon, the late Dr. Harry Chun-Hoon, Dr. Albert and Myrna Chun-Hoon, Lawrence and Frances Ching; Herbert and Alma Ho, Merle Chong, Sam and Muriel Wong, Elaine Yee, Robert and Velma Akinaka, Melvin Kau and Kara Zen.

I would also like to express my gratitude to Dr. Lee Winters and Gael Mustapha for their help in preparing and editing the preliminary drafts; to Frances Matsumoto for secretarial assistance; to Lawrence Ing for his outstanding illustrations; to Zhao Wang Zhou for his elegant calligraphy; to the Hawaii Chinese History Center, its president, Roger K. S. Liu, and its executive director, Puanani K. Woo, for being willing to publish this book; and to the University of Hawaii Press, especially Iris Wiley and Stuart Kiang, for helping make this book a reality.

Finally, special thanks to my wife, Marjorie, who helped in so many ways. Her suggestions and constant encouragement were invaluable.

Echoes from Old China

Pan Ku

CHAPTER 1

Chinese Origins

Interestingly, while there are myths and legends which describe creation and the dawn of Chinese culture, the true origin of the Chinese remains unknown. Archaeology has shed a little light on the earliest cultures in China but has not solved this perplexing riddle.

Mythical Origins

Pan Ku

According to legend, in the beginning there was only darkness and chaos. Then an extremely large egg appeared, called the Great Monad. This vast egg was subjected to two opposing forces or principles. The interaction of the two forces—yin 陰, the passive or negative female principle, and yang 陽, the active or positive male principle—caused the egg to produce Pan Ku 盤古 and the shell to separate. The upper half of the shell formed the heavens, and the lower half the earth.

Pan Ku has been depicted in many ways. He sometimes appears as a dwarf with two horns on his head, clothed in skin or leaves. He may be holding a hammer in one hand and a chisel in the other, or perhaps the symbol of yin and yang. He may also be shown holding the sun in one hand and the moon in the other. He is often depicted with his companions the four supernatural animals—the phoenix, the dragon, the unicorn and the tortoise. In any case, Pan Ku grew rapidly and increased his height by six to ten feet daily. He hammered and chiseled a massive piece of granite floating aimlessly in space, and as he worked, the heavens and the earth became progressively wider. He labored ceaselessly for eighteen thousand years and his body dissolved when his work was done.

Following his death, his head became the mountains, his breath the wind and clouds, his voice the thunder; his left eye became the sun and his right eye the moon. His beard became the stars, his four limbs the four quadrants of the globe, his blood the rivers and his veins and muscles the layers of the earth. His flesh became the soil, his skin and hair became the trees and plants, his seminal fluid became pearls and his marrow precious stones. His sweat turned into rain, and the parasites on his body, impregnated by the wind, began the human race.

Through his great labor, Pan Ku divided chaos into yin, represented by the Royal

1

Mother of the West 西王母, and yang, represented by the Duke of the East 東王公. These two principles gave birth to the Heavenly Emperors, who were followed by the Earthly Emperors, the ancestors of the Chinese rulers. The Five Perfect Earthly Emperors were Fu Hsi 伏羲, Shen Nung 神農, Huang Ti 黃帝, Yao 堯 and Shun 舜.

Fu Hsi

Fu Hsi, the first of the Five Perfect Earthly Emperors, is said to have reigned from 2953 to 2838 B.C. He was born in the province of Shensi 陝西 and, according to legend, was carried in his mother's womb for twelve years before birth. He taught people how to hunt, fish, domesticate animals and tend their flocks. He instituted marriage and taught people how to devise tools to split wood, kindle fire and cook food. He devised the Eight Trigrams 八卦, which evolved from markings on tortoise shells. These trigrams served as the basis for mathematics, medicine, divination and geomancy, and as clues to the secrets of creation such as the evolution of nature and its cyclic changes.

Eight Trigrams

Shen Nung

Shen Nung, the Divine Farmer, followed Fu Hsi and reigned from 2838 to 2698 B.C. According to legend, Shen Nung was conceived through the influence of the Heavenly Dragon. He is credited with inventing the wooden plow and teaching people the art of agriculture. By experimenting with various plants, he discovered which plants were useful and which plants were harmful or poisonous. He also expanded the system of eight trigrams into sixty-four hexagrams.

Huang Ti, Fu Hsi and Shen Nung

Huang Ti

Huang Ti, the Yellow Emperor, reigned from 2698 to 2598 B.C. He is said to have had full command of the language while still an infant.

Huang Ti invented the wheel and discovered the art of making pottery. He improved communication by building roads, bridges and ships. He divided time into sixty-year cycles 花甲子 and organized his empire in units of ten—that is, ten towns made up a village, ten villages a district, ten districts a province, and ten provinces constituted the empire.

His consort, Lady Hsi Ling 西陵氏, is credited with developing the art of sericulture —the raising of silkworms and the methods of silk production. She also taught people the art of weaving.

Yao

Yao, who was born with eyebrows of eight different colors, is said to have reigned beginning in 2356 B.C. Under his direction, his court astronomers determined the dates of the sol-stice and equinox, added days and months to adjust the lunar calendar and fixed the four seasons so that farmers might know when to plant and harvest crops.

After ruling for seventy years, he relinquished his throne and selected Shun, instead of his own son, to be the next emperor. He also gave his two daughters, Nu Ying 女英 and O-Huang 娥皇, in marriage to Shun.

Shun

Shun, a native of Honan 河南 province, was unusually gifted physically and mentally. He is described as having had two pupils in each eye.

Shun was disliked intensely by his father, stepmother and stepbrother, who tried to kill him on two occasions. Once, while Shun was

Yao

Shun

working on a roof, they removed the ladder and set the house on fire. Later, when he was working in a well, they attempted to bury him alive. Both times he managed to escape unharmed. Despite their attempts on his life, Shun always demonstrated extreme devotion and filial piety toward his father and stepmother. It was because of this virtue, as well as others, that Yao selected Shun as his successor. Shun's reign extended to 2255 B.C.

Anthropological Origins

Peking Man

For centuries, the people in the village of Choukoutien 周口店, situated about thirty miles southwest of Peking, had been digging up "dragon bones." These fossil bones were pulverized and used in various medicines.

Early in the twentieth century, a fossilized molar found at Choukoutien was shown to Dr. Davidson Black, a Canadian physician who was teaching anatomy at Peking Union Medical College. Black was interested in anthropology and had previously worked in England helping to restore the skull of the Piltdown Man, supposedly an early genus and species of man which later proved to be a hoax. After studying the size and cusp pattern of the fossil tooth, Black concluded that since it was clearly not from a higher ape or from a modern man, or *Homo sapiens*, it could only be from a very early man. From the evidence of this single tooth, he announced the discovery of a new genus of man, *Sinanthropus pekinesis*—the Peking Man.

With funding from the Rockefeller Foundation, scientific excavation under Black's direction began in 1927 at a cave in Choukoutien. Excavation of the hard limestone cave was difficult and painstaking as tons and tons of earth were carefully dug, sifted and examined. In 1934, Black suffered a fatal heart attack.

Dr. Franz Weidenreich, a visiting professor of anatomy at the University of Chicago, was selected to take over the project. The excavation at Choukoutien was unique at the time because it was a vertical dig extending to a depth of about 160 feet. This enabled the scientists to study the history of the cave and discover clues as to how the Peking Man lived. Parts of 45 skeletons were uncovered, including pieces from 14 skulls and 14 lower jaws, 150 teeth and bones of 14 children. In addition, there were bones from 60 different animals, tools made from quartz and flintlike stones, plant fibers, seeds and evidence of a hearth. At the bottom of the cave, bones of carnivorous animals and human layers alternated fairly regularly. Toward the top, there were only human remains. From this evidence scientists deduced that large carnivorous animals such as saber-toothed tigers and huge hyenas, now extinct, had originally inhabited the cave. Later, the Peking Man drove them out and occupied it.

By studying the bones, the scientists concluded that Peking Man lived about 500,000 years ago. He was about 5 feet tall, and his brain volume was approximately 1,000 cc. By comparison, the average brain volume of the higher ape is 450 cc. and that of modern man is 1,300 cc. Apes have a relatively small head and a large face while modern men have a relatively large head and a small face. The head/face ratio of Peking Man was between the two. He had a broad nose, a sloping forehead, massive brow ridges and no chin. He walked upright, could run and probably could talk. He was mainly a flesh eater. Both large and small animals were part of his diet, but his favorite food was ven-

Head of the Peking Man (reconstructed)

American ship, the *President Harrison*, berthed at Chingwantao 秦皇島, a port north of Tientsin 天津, for shipment to the United States. On December 7 (December 8 in Asia), Pearl Harbor was attacked and war was declared between Japan and the United States. The *President Harrison* was beached, and the special train carrying the collection of bones was seized by the Japanese.

Somehow the bones of Peking Man disappeared, raising a number of questions that still remain unanswered. Were the bones hidden or buried in China so as to prevent the Japanese from stealing them? Were they hidden in Japan? Were they on a Japanese ship which was sunk while en route to Japan?

Since the end of World War II, several nations have tried to find the bones. The Looted Properties Division of the Far East Command searched everywhere in Japan but was unable to locate them. Dr. W. C. Pei 裴文中, who discovered the first skull of the Peking Man at Choukoutien, charged that the bones were stolen by the American Museum of Natural History in New York. However, Dr. Harry L. Shapiro, chairman of the museum's anthropology department, claimed that the museum had only the casts of the fossils. The casts had been sent to the museum by Dr. Weidenreich prior to World War II. To date, the riddle of the missing bones of Peking Man remains unsolved.

Neolithic Cultures

Fragmentary evidence suggests that, after the time of the Peking Man, early man lived in many regions of Central Asia and China. One of the regions was the Ordos area of Inner

ison. He also ate plants and grains. Evidence from the clay in the cave and charred bones suggest that he used fire.

In the fall of 1941, war between the United States and Japan appeared inevitable. Japan was completing its occupation of China and was on the brink of conquering the countries of Southeast Asia as well. While Dr. Weidenreich was visiting the United States, the Geological Survey of the Netherlands East Indies requested that the irreplaceable bones of Peking Man be sent to the United States for safekeeping. A detachment of U.S. Marines left Peking on a special train at 5 a.m. on December 5, 1941. Their mission was to deliver the bones to an

Mongolia, which was inhabited around 50,000 B.C. Also, in the upper layers of the Choukoutien cave dating from around 25,000 B.C. were found suggestions of a non-mongol race which may be related to the Ainu of northern Japan.

Yangshao Culture

The first evidence of a neolithic culture in China was discovered at Yangshao 仰韶, in Honan province, in 1921. In 1953, during construction of a factory at Pan-po 半坡, near the city of Sian 西安 in Shensi province, a neolithic village belonging to the Yangshao culture was accidentally uncovered. This village covered an area of two and a half acres. Careful excavation revealed the presence of 45 houses, 200 storage pits, needles, tools, arrowheads, fish hooks and six kilns. There were also 174 adult graves, 76 children's graves and 37 funerary urns. The neolithic people of Pan-po hunted, fished, cultivated millet, cooked their food and raised pigs as domestic animals.

Red pottery

Especially noteworthy was their gray or red pottery. The red pottery was painted with black geometrical designs and occasionally with pictures of fish or human faces. Because the potter's wheel was unknown at that time, the vessels were probably fashioned with strips of clay. The Yangshao culture, also referred to as the "Painted Pottery" culture, flourished between 6000 and 5000 B.C.

The excavation site in Pan-po and a museum were opened to visitors in 1958.

Lungshan Culture

In 1928, another neolithic culture was discovered at Lungshan 龍山, in Shantung 山東 province. The Lungshan culture was more advanced than the Yangshao culture and probably flourished about a thousand years later, between 5000 and 4000 B.C. People of the Lungshan culture also hunted, fished and planted grain. They probably domesticated the pig, dog and ox. They made tools such as axes and knives as well as necklaces and bracelets. They also made a black pottery, probably with the potter's wheel. Their pottery was not painted but was decorated with rings, either raised or grooved.

The Lungshan culture, because of its distinguished pottery, has been called the "Black Pottery" culture. It was probably the predecessor of the Hsia 夏 and Shang 商 dynasties.

Recent research has persuaded some authorities that the Yangshao and Lungshan cultures were not separate and distinct. These scholars now believe that the Lungshan culture was in fact a later development of the Yangshao culture.

Brief Chronology of Chinese Dynasties

Legendary Period

Five Perfect Earthly Emperors	c. 2953–2255 B.C.
Fu Hsi 伏義	2953–2838
Shen Nung 神農	2838–2698
Huang Ti 黃帝	2698–2598
Yao 堯 and Shun 舜	2356–2255

Historical Period

Hsia 夏	c. 21st–16th century B.C.
Shang 商	c. 16th–11th century B.C.
Chou 周	c. 11th century–221 B.C.
Spring and Autumn 春秋	771–475 B.C.
Warring States 戰國	475–221 B.C.
Chin 秦	221–206 B.C.
Han 漢	206 B.C.–A.D. 220
China Divided	A.D. 220–589
Three Kingdoms 三國	220–280
Six Dynasties 六朝	265–589
Sui 隋	589–618
Tang 唐	618–906
Five Dynasties 五代	907–960
Sung 宋	960–1279
Yuan 元	1279–1368
Ming 明	1368–1644
Hung Wu 洪武	1368–1398
Chien Wen 建文	1399–1402
Yung Lo 永樂	1403–1424
Hung Hsi 洪熙	1425
Hsuan Te 宣德	1426–1435
Cheng Tung 正統	1436–1449
Ching Tai 景泰	1450–1457
Tien Shun 天順	1457–1464
Cheng Hua 成花	1465–1487
Hung Chih 弘治	1488–1505
Cheng Te 正德	1506–1521
Chia Ching 嘉靖	1522–1566
Lung Ching 隆慶	1567–1572
Wan Li 萬歷	1573–1620
Tai Chang 泰昌	1620
Tien Chi 天啟	1621–1627
Chung Cheng 崇禎	1628–1644
Ching 清	1644–1911
Shun Chih 順治	1644–1661
Kang Hsi 康熙	1662–1722
Yung Cheng 雍正	1723–1735
Chien Lung 乾隆	1736–1796
Chia Ching 嘉慶	1796–1821
Tao Kuang 道光	1821–1850
Hsien Feng 咸豐	1851–1861
Tung Chih 同治	1862–1873
Kuang Hsu 光緒	1874–1908
Hsuan Tung 宣統	1908–1911
Republic of China 中華民國	1911–1949
People's Republic of China 中華人民共和國	1949–Present

CHAPTER 2

Chinese Ways

Since the cultures of China and non-Asiatic countries stem from different backgrounds, it is not surprising that their philosophies, customs, traditions, codes, costumes and behaviors developed in quite dissimilar ways. At times, however, these differences have led to confusion and misunderstandings, prompting the inevitable remark that the Chinese are inscrutable.

But how are the Chinese different from other peoples? What were some of the customs peculiar to the Chinese? Let us start with clothing. Both sexes wore jackets and trousers in old China, and men often wore long robes or long skirts. Men also wore long stockings, while women wore socks. Gloves were not worn in cold weather. Instead, people used the long, large sleeves of their robes and jackets as muffs to ward off the winter's cold and to keep their hands warm.

Many women had extremely small feet, sometimes measuring only several inches in length. The curious Chinese custom of footbinding probably began during the Tang 唐 dynasty, around A.D. 900. To produce the abnormality, girls' feet were bound during early childhood when they were still quite flex-

ible. Tiny feet were considered not only erotic but the mark of a well-bred, well-to-do and refined woman. Although footbinding was painful, disfiguring and crippling, it remained in vogue for many centuries. It remained popular even during the Ching 清 dynasty (1644–1911) despite the many attempts that were made to ban it. It was not until the late 1800s and the

Bound feet with embroidered shoes

emancipation of women in China that this cruel practice gradually began to disappear.

In old China, the wearing of jewelry was not confined to women. Older men frequently wore expensive jade bracelets and a long string of beads around their neck. It was also common for men to carry folding fans, which was not seen as a sign of effeminacy. A man who did so was a man of culture.

When meeting, men did not shake hands. Instead, each clasped his own hands, raised them to the level of the lower chest and then moved them up and down a few inches several times. When meeting an individual of superior rank, an inferior bowed reverently and raised his clasped hands to the forehead several times in order to show politeness and respect. Women, too, did not clasp hands when meeting but instead lightly grasped the end of their long left sleeve with the right hand and carried out the same motions.

People in China commonly greeted each other by saying, "Have you eaten your rice?" This might seem a strange remark if taken literally, but the Chinese thought nothing of asking personal questions which many Westerners would consider rude, insulting or excessively inquisitive. For example, a Chinese would not hesitate to ask a perfect stranger, How old are you? Who is your father? Where is your ancestral village? Are you married? How do you write your name? Where are you going? What are you going to do there? Where do you work? How much do you earn? How much did you pay for your house?

Similarly, when one said, "Oh! You have gotten fatter," it was considered a compliment indicating that the person must be in good health and eating well. Conversely, when one said, "Oh! You have gotten thinner," it was

Men greeting each other

taken as an expression of concern over the possibility that the person might be ill and unable to eat well.

On parting, the Chinese did not say, "Goodbye." Instead, they used the common expression "Please walk slowly" or "Have a good walk home."

During a friendly visit, hot tea was served instead of coffee or alcohol. The tea was served and received with both hands, and sipped throughout the visit.

When conducting business at a government official's home, the citizen doffed his hat before entering. The official put on his official cap decorated with the button of his rank when he greeted a visitor at the door. If his servant served the visitor tea, he let him place it on the tea stand and paid no particular attention to it. However, if the official offered the tea personally, it was considered courteous to rise and receive it with both hands. The tea was then placed on the tea stand and not sipped.

When talking to one whose position and rank were much higher, a supplicant could not look into the official's eyes but instead directed his gaze to the region of the official's left breast, only occasionally glancing to his face. When the official nodded and softly said, "Yes," this did not mean that he necessarily agreed. It merely meant that he was listening and following the logic or that he understood. When the official wanted to conclude the discussion, he touched his tea cup with his fingers and hoped that the visitor would recognize the hint. At the conclusion of the visit, the visitor would invite his host to drink the tea with him before leaving.

At dinner, the place of honor was to the left of the host. At large dinners, it was common for men to sit together at one table while the women occupied another separate table. There were no knives and forks on the tables, and chopsticks were used to convey food from the plate or bowl to the mouth. Bowls and cups could be raised to the mouth for eating and drinking, but plates remained on the table. A gracious host would apologize for serving "rough tea" and "tasteless rice" even when the food served was rare and sumptuous. A good host, moreover, would encourage his guests to do away with formality and to drink the warm wine without restraint. For their part, guests were careful not to select all the choicest morsels or pile the food on their plates or bowls.

When dinner was finished, the chopsticks were placed across the bowl. The host again apologized and implored his guests, "If the food was not good, please at least fill yourself with rice before leaving." Then, instead of finger bowls, warm, moist hand towels were presented to allow the fingers, hands and mouth to be cleaned.

Whenever things were presented or received in China, no matter how large or small, both hands were used. It was considered rude if only one hand was used, especially the left hand.

Chinese hand gestures differed greatly from those of Western cultures. To signify "number one" or the best, the Chinese clenched the right fist and raised the thumb, not the index finger. The hand gesture for beckoning was to extend the fingers in a raking motion while flexing the elbow. To emphasize no, the opened right hand was raised close to the shoulder and moved slightly from side to side instead of extending the right arm in front of the body and moving the hand from side to side.

Young men in China were clean shaven and were not permitted to sprout mustaches or beards. Only after age forty-five were men allowed to cultivate mustaches. After age sixty, they were allowed to grow beards. Indeed, they were allowed to let mustaches and beards grow as long as they wished.

It is well known that the Chinese revered old age. The older the man, the more respect he was accorded, for it was believed that as a man aged, he acquired precious experience and wisdom.

Calendar dates were identified by the year, month and day instead of the month, day and year. Bright red was the color for rejoicing and happiness. The colors for mourning were white, gray or blue, not black.

In printing and writing, the Chinese characters were aligned vertically from top to bottom and from right to left. Books were also paged from right to left. The title of a book was written not only on the front cover but frequently on the spine and on the bottom. Books printed on soft paper were stored on the shelf horizontally, exposing either the spine or the bottom. Strips of paper serving as bookmarks were placed at the lower edge of the book.

The Chinese did not develop an alphabet. Characters in the dictionary were classified under one of 214 radicals or roots and arranged according to the number of strokes. All the characters were monosyllabic, so that even with tonal variations and inflections the number of available sounds was limited. A particular sound might therefore correspond to many different characters, depending on the context. If the word or meaning was not clear, the character was then written or outlined on the palm, table top or in the air with the index finger or with a closed folding fan.

There was no word for brother, sister, uncle, aunt or other general kinship designations. The term used was very specific and depended on whether the individual in question was older or younger and also whether the relationship was paternal or maternal. Similarly, there was no general character for rice. Specific characters were used to describe each state of growth and the condition of the rice—whether it was husked or unhusked and whether it was cooked or uncooked.

The character for religion was the same as the character meaning "to teach." There was no character for the word China. The Chinese called their country the "Middle Kingdom" 中國.

An individual's title followed instead of preceded his or her name. For example, Mr. Chao was Chao, Mr. 趙先生. Miss Chien was Chien, Miss 錢小姐. And Dr. Sun was Sun, Dr. 孫醫生.

The magnetic compass was said to point south instead of north, and so it was called the "Pointing South Needle" 指南針.

For arithmetic and business calculations, the Chinese relied on the abacus, a frame with sliding beads. Fractions were expressed differently—for example, one-fourth was "one of four parts."

The carpenter's saw blade was set on a wooden frame. The carpenter's plane was pulled toward his body rather than being pushed away from it. In needlework, the needle was placed over the thread instead of the thread through the needle.

Finally, unlike Westerners, the Chinese did not place much emphasis on personal independence and freedom. They were willing to sacrifice these qualities for the good of the family and clan. Indeed, too much independence and freedom was considered a form of selfishness.

CHAPTER 3

Chinese Names

Chinese names generally consist of three characters. The first character is the surname. The following two characters, taken together, constitute the given name. The first character of the given name is usually an adjective modifying the second character, a noun.

It is often claimed that there are approximately 500 surnames in China. This belief seems to derive from a well-known text titled *One Hundred Family Surnames* 百家姓, written by an unknown author during the Sung 宋 dynasty (960–1279). This book was used widely as a vocabulary text for students in old China, and it lists 507 surnames, of which 441 consist of one character and 66 consist of two characters. This list, however, is by no means exhaustive. At present, there are more than 5,000 Chinese surnames. They are derived from many sources, such as the names of ancient states or townships, official titles, given names, posthumous names, and specific localities or trades.

The most common surnames in China, in descending order, are Chao 趙, Chien 錢, Sun 孫, Li 李, Chou 周, Wu 吳, Cheng 鄭 and Wang 王. In southern China, however, the most common names, in the order of frequency, are Chen 陳, Li 李, Chang 張, Huang 黃, Ho 何, Wu 吳, Chou 周, Hu 胡, Ma 馬 and Mai 麥.

In old China, one's surname was revered because the individual bearing it was but a small link in the long history of an illustrious clan. One never changed a name, especially a surname. If a person did so, he or she had probably committed a grave and heinous crime and wanted to sever ties with the past through a name change. Such a person would most likely move away from home to start life anew.

People with the same surname shared a commonality and considered themselves relatives regardless of the number of generations removed, the geographical distance or lack of consanguinity. Since the commonality was derived from a common ancestor at some point in time, it was considered an insult when a person with the same surname disclaimed family or other close relationships. For the same reason, old Chinese custom prohibited marriages of couples with the same surname.

A Chinese had many given names. One month after birth, an infant was given a "milk name" 乳名. This name was used by family members, relatives and close friends. The name was usually selected either by the family elder or by a literate friend. Names for boys reflected the parents' wishes for his good health, longevity, prosperity, expected talents, virtues, diligence, filial piety, patriotism or intelligence. Girls were named after exotic flowers, pretty birds, musical instruments or jewels. Girls might also be named for feminine attributes such as beauty, grace, thrift and purity. In some families, however, girls were not given names but were simply referred to as the "oldest girl" 大妹, "second girl" 二妹, "third girl" 三妹 and so forth.

Frequently, all the boys in one family would be given names that shared the same first character, or adjective. This was sometimes done with the girls in the family as well. Since the two characters of the given name go together, they should be spelled together as a single word or hyphenated when the name is anglicized.

Another method for selecting a given name was based on the child's horoscope and its relationship to the "Five Elements" 五行. A fortune teller, after studying the month, day and hour of the birth, determined whether the infant had a full complement of the Five Elements of metal 金, wood 木, water 水, fire 火 and earth 土. If any element was lacking in the child, a character with the radical or root of the missing element was used in the name to correct the deficiency and make the child "complete." For example, if the child was lacking water, he might be given the name Hai 海, meaning "ocean," because that character is based on the water radical 氵.

Characters totalling eighteen or nineteen strokes were to be avoided in a given name. It was claimed that such a name would have an adverse effect on the life of an individual, predisposing him or her to misfortune, poor health and an early death.

At home, among close relatives and good friends, the prefix Ya 亞 was often used informally to replace the first character of the "milk name." This prefix has no meaning and was used to make the name more euphonic. For example, if a boy's name was Kuei-An 貴安, meaning "precious peace," he might be called Ya-An 亞安, or Peace.

There were no "Juniors" in Chinese names. A son was never named after his father, nor did parents name their children after relatives. Each child was considered an entirely separate individual. When a boy enrolled in school, he was given a "school name" 學名 or "book name" 書名. This name was used by his teachers and schoolmates and alluded to his intelligence, diligence or scholarship.

After marriage, the clan bestowed a young man with his "style name" 名字. The first character, or adjective, of the two-character style name was the same for all the married men of that particular generation of the clan. The second character, the noun, was not duplicated. This name became his formal name.

In old China, it was considered improper for a married woman to reveal or use her given name. For example, if her maiden surname was Li 李 and she was married to a man whose surname was Wang 王, she called herself Wang-Li Shih 王李氏, which meant Mrs. Wang née Li.

Nicknames 花名 were common. These names were often based on a physical defect, a peculiarity in personality or an unusual incident in the individual's life. A nickname was usually accepted gracefully and used by others without hostility.

Writers, artists and actors had "special names" 別號 that were equivalent to pen names or studio names. A scholar who passed the old imperial civil service examination and became a government official was given an "official name" 官名. Some important people were given a "posthumous name" 謚號, and a deceased emperor was usually granted a "temple name" 廟名.

Anglicization of Chinese names has created

much confusion, for a name might be spelled in many ways depending on the dialect spoken and how the translator interpreted the sound of the name. Moreover, although Chinese write their surname first and then the two characters of the given name, as in a directory or name file, many Westerners assumed that the last character was the surname. In time, through common Western usage, some Chinese have even replaced their surname with the anglicized given name.

Some Chinese living abroad have also changed their surnames and given names to conform with names used in their adopted countries. In the United States, for example, the surname Ho 何 has been changed to Holt, Lo 羅 has become Loew, Hsieh 謝 has become Shea and Chung 鍾 has become June.

CHAPTER 4

The Chinese Lunar-Solar Calendar

According to legend, the Chinese started to compute time from 2698 B.C., during the reign of the Yellow Emperor, Huang Ti 黃帝, when his prime minister devised a system of "sixty-year cycles" 花甲子. In the twenty-third century B.C., the Perfect Emperor Yao 堯 commanded his astronomers to observe the solstice and equinox and fix the dates of the four seasons so that farmers might know when to plant their seeds and harvest their crops.

The evidence suggests that the Chinese used a gnomon, a crude sun dial, to determine the solstice and equinox some time before the twelfth century B.C. This simple instrument was a vertical pole about eight feet in height set vertically in the ground. By measuring the length of the sun's shadow cast by the pole, the solstice (the longest and shortest days of the year) and the equinox (when days and nights are of equal length) were determined.

By the time of the Han 漢 dynasty (206 B.C.–A.D. 220), enough data had been accumulated for the principles of the calendar to be formulated. A year was divided into days and lunar months. A lunar month consisted of 29.53 days, the time required for the moon to make one complete revolution around the earth.

Consequently, a year made up of twelve lunar months was not 365.25 days (the time for the earth to completely circumnavigate the sun), but only 354.3 days—about eleven days shorter than a year in the Gregorian calendar 陽曆. The lunar calendar 陰曆 therefore required periodic adjustment. This was accomplished by adding a day or a month to the calendar when the cumulative fractions equaled a complete unit—a process termed "intercalation."

Adjusting the lunar calendar, then, meant adding an extra day about every two months, since a lunar month was 29.53 days. Thus, some lunar months had 29 days and others had 30 days. To correct the deficiency of eleven days a year, a lunar month was added every three years. This added month was called an "intercalary month" 閏月, and it could be inserted in the calendar after any month except the first, eleventh and twelfth months. With the addition of the intercalary month, that particular year would then be composed of thirteen lunar months and was termed a "complete year."

In the lunar calendar, the first day of the month coincides with the new moon, and the middle of the month, the fifteenth day, usually coincides with the full moon. The new year arrives with the second new moon following the winter solstice, and since the winter solstice falls on or about December 22, the lunar New Year comes between January 21 and February 20. The second moon—that is, the second lunar month—must include the vernal or spring equinox (March 21), the fifth moon the summer solstice (June 21), the eighth moon the autumn equinox (September 23) and the eleventh moon the winter solstice. The four seasons in the lunar calendar are considered to begin about six weeks earlier than their counterparts in the Gregorian calendar. The beginning of spring usually occurs during the first moon, the beginning of summer during the fourth moon, the beginning of autumn during the seventh moon and the beginning of winter during the tenth moon.

By the eighth century B.C., the Chinese had calculated that within a period of 19 years, there were a total of 235 moons, of which 7 were intercalary moons. They discovered that the phases of the moon recurred on the same day of the calendar every 19 years. This recurrent astronomical cycle is known as the Metonic Cycle, named after Meton, a Greek astronomer who discovered the same phenomenon some four centuries later, in the fourth century B.C.

When compared to the Gregorian calendar, dates in the lunar calendar vary considerably from year to year, making it an unreliable guide for planting and harvesting. To make it more useful for the farmer, twenty-four "joints" 節 and "breaths" 氣 were incorporated in the calendar, spaced about every two weeks throughout the year. These joints and breaths were based on the position of the sun, and were used to designate the days of the solstice and equinox and to describe the climatic conditions of north China around the area of the Yellow River, or Huang Ho 黃河. Referred to as the Farmer's Calendar 農歷, they became a reliable guide for the farmer's planting and harvesting of crops.

Farmer's Calendar (Joints and Breaths)	*Gregorian Calendar* (Approximate date)
1. Beginning of Spring 立春 The Beginning of Spring was usually in the first moon. At times, when the lunar new year came after February 6, there was no Beginning of Spring. This was a so-called blind year 盲年. In such a year it would not be auspicious to enroll a child in school. If the Beginning of Spring was clear and bright, plowing would be easy.	February 6
2. Rain Water 雨水 This was the time of the spring rains.	February 19
3. Awakening of Insects 驚蟄 On this day the insects appeared and thunder could be expected.	March 6
4. Spring Equinox 春分 The day was as long as the night. Rain was a good omen.	March 21
5. Clear and Bright 清明 This was the true Spring Festival, the first festival for the dead. People visited the graves and honored the spirits of their ancestors. If the south winds blew, the harvest would be good.	April 5
6. Grain Rain 穀雨 It was time to sow the wheat.	April 20

7. Beginning of Summer 立夏   May 5
   The beginning of the summer heat.

8. Slight Filling 小滿   May 21
   Wheat sown the previous autumn was beginning to fill its ears.

9. Grain in the Ear 芒種   June 6
   The end of the sowing season. A thunder storm on this day was a good omen.

10. Summer Solstice 夏至   June 21
    The longest day of the year, a time to dig up the garlic.

11. Slight Heat 小暑   July 7
    The beginning of humid, sultry weather.

12. Great Heat 大暑   July 23
    If exceedingly hot, the five grains would be of good quality.

13. Beginning of Autumn 立秋   August 8
    Hot and humid weather persist.

14. End of Heat 處暑   August 21
    Summer was over.

15. White Dew 白露   September 8
    Dry weather. Time to sow the winter wheat that would be harvested in the fourth moon.

16. Autumn Equinox 秋分   September 23
    Good weather meant a good harvest.

17. Cold Dew 寒露   October 8
    Leaves begin to fall.

18. Frost Descends 霜降   October 23
    Expect frost and ice.

19. Beginning of Winter 立冬   November 7
20. Slight Snow 小雪   November 21
21. Great Snow 大雪   December 7
22. Winter Solstice 冬至   December 22
    The shortest day of the year.
23. Slight Cold 小寒   January 6
24. Great Cold 大寒   January 21

The Chinese frequently named years according to the year of an emperor's reign. For example, 1900 was the twenty-sixth year of Emperor Kuang Hsu 光緒, whose reign began in 1874. Another method for naming years derived from combinations of the "ten celestial stems" 十天干 with the "twelve terrestrial branches" 十二地支, represented by twelve animals. The name of a year was composed of two characters, the first being one of the ten celestial stems and the other, one of the twelve terrestrial branches. The stems and branches were arranged in chronological order and repeated. Thus the name of a particular year did not recur until sixty years had passed; on the sixty-first year, the cycle repeated itself.

The ten celestial stems, twelve terrestrial branches and twelve animals representing the branches are as follows:

Ten Celestial Stems	Twelve Terrestrial Branches	Twelve Animals
1. Chia 甲	1. Tzu 子	1. Rat
2. Yi 乙	2. Chou 丑	2. Ox
3. Ping 丙	3. Yin 寅	3. Tiger
4. Ting 丁	4. Mao 卯	4. Hare
5. Wu 戊	5. Chen 辰	5. Dragon
6. Chi 己	6. Ssu 巳	6. Snake
7. Keng 庚	7. Wu 午	7. Horse
8. Hsin 辛	8. Wei 未	8. Sheep
9. Jen 壬	9. Shen 申	9. Monkey
10. Kwei 癸	10. Yu 酉	10. Fowl
1. Chia 甲	11. Hsu 戌	11. Dog
2. Yi 乙	12. Hai 亥	12. Pig
3. Ping 丙	1. Tzu 子	1. Rat
4. Ting 丁	2. Chou 丑	2. Ox
5. Wu 戊 . . .	3. Yin 寅 . . .	3. Tiger. . .

For example, 1984 was the Chia-Tzu 甲子 year, the year of the Rat. The following year was the Yi-Chou 乙丑 year, the year of the Ox.

The thirteenth year of the cycle, 1996, will be the Ping-Tzu 丙子 year, again the year of the Rat. After the completion of a sixty-year cycle in 2043, the cycle will repeat itself with the Chia-Tzu year in 2044.

A day in old China was divided into twelve two-hour watches. The two-hour watches were also named after the twelve terrestrial branches and the twelve animals:

Time	Twelve Terrestrial Branches	Twelve Animals
11 p.m. to 1 a.m.	Tzu 子	Rat
1 to 3	Chou 丑	Ox
3 to 5	Yin 寅	Tiger
5 to 7	Mao 卯	Hare
7 to 9	Chen 辰	Dragon
9 to 11	Ssu 巳	Snake
11 a.m. to 1 p.m.	Wu 午	Horse
1 to 3	Wei 未	Sheep
3 to 5	Shen 申	Monkey
5 to 7	Yu 酉	Fowl
7 to 9	Hsu 戌	Dog
9 to 11 p.m.	Hai 亥	Pig

For centuries, the preparation of the new lunar calendar was a major function of the imperial government. A special board of mathematicians headed by a minister prepared it, and the new calendar was submitted to the emperor for approval. He was considered the "mediator between Heaven and Earth" and the "regulator of the seasons." With pomp and ceremony at the imperial palace, the emperor then presented the new calendar to the country. It was a major crime, punishable by death, for anyone to issue a new calendar independently.

The Gregorian calendar was officially adopted by China following the revolution in 1911. However, the Chinese people still use the dates of the lunar-solar calendar for celebrating most of their festivals. The biggest holiday in the People's Republic of China is still the lunar New Year, renamed the Spring Festival. Old traditions obviously have been slow to change.

CHAPTER 5

Celebrations and Festivals

A peasant in China, weather permitting, worked every day in the fields plowing, sowing, planting, watering, fertilizing, weeding and harvesting crops. The farmer also tended ducks, chickens, pigs and water buffalo. There were no Sabbaths, no half-days off, no weekends off, and no scheduled vacations to interrupt the work cycle. But this did not mean the peasant had no time for rest and recreation. There were many celebrations and festivals throughout the year, affording opportunities to leave the work in the fields and to rest and enjoy life. There were weddings and birthday celebrations to attend as well as funeral services of relatives and friends. The Chinese also observed the changing of the seasons by performing the proper rites and ceremonies, and honored historical personages and a host of deities. These celebrations were family, temple or community affairs.

There were six major festivals and many minor ones. Among the major festivals, three were for the living 人節 and three were for the dead 鬼節. The three festivals for the living were the lunar New Year 元旦, the Fifth Moon Festival 五月節 and the Mid-Autumn Festival 中秋節. Three times a year, before the three festivals for the living, debtors settled their arrears. The three festivals for the dead were the Clear and Bright 清明, the Fourteenth Day of the Seventh Moon 七月十四節 and the Double-Nine 重陽節.

The six major festivals and some of the popular minor ones are listed and described below. A number of these festivals are still celebrated today in China and by Chinese in other countries:

Festival	Date
Lunar New Year	1st day of the 1st moon
Lantern	15th day of the 1st moon
Birthday of the Local Earth God	2nd day of the 2nd moon
Birthday of the Goddess of Mercy	19th day of the 2nd moon
Clear and Bright	2nd or 3rd moon
Birthday of Buddha	8th day of the 4th moon
Fifth Moon	5th day of the 5th moon
Birthday of the God of War	13th day of the 5th moon
Worship of the Seven Sisters	7th day of the 7th moon
Fourteenth Day of the Seventh Moon	14th day of the 7th moon
Mid-Autumn	15th day of the 8th moon
Double-Nine	9th day of the 9th moon
Winter Solstice	11th moon

19

The Lunar New Year Festival

In the lunar calendar, New Year's Day 元旦 is the first day of the second moon following the winter solstice 冬至. It usually falls between January 21 and February 20.

Preparations for the New Year

Preparations for the New Year Festival would begin in the twelfth lunar month.

Everyone in the family helped to make glutinous rice flour 糯米粉. The raw glutinous rice was first washed and partially dried. The rice was then pounded in a stone or cement mortar with a heavy iron pole used as a pestle. The flour produced was sifted, dried on round, flat bamboo trays and then stored in containers. This flour was used to make the New Year's puddings 年糕 and other delicacies such as dumplings, crullers and deep fried round "doughnuts" 煎堆 which were filled with black bean paste or with crushed roasted unsalted peanuts and shredded coconut.

The Hakka 客家 people are famous for their puffed rice cakes 通米. People who made these cakes cooked the glutinous rice by steaming. The grains of cooked rice were then separated, sun dried and later puffed in hot sand. Unsalted peanuts were also roasted. When ready to be made into rice cakes, the roasted peanuts were added to the puffed rice and the mixture was spread evenly on a bamboo tray. A hot syrup made with sugar, a little honey and spiced with ginger root was poured over the rice. When made correctly, the syrup caramelized and bound the rice. The sheet of rice was then cut into bite-size cakes.

In inexperienced hands, the syrup might not be made properly and, when poured over the rice, would not caramelize and bind the rice. This was usually the result of too little sugar being used or perhaps too high a heat in the preparation of the syrup, causing the solution to be supersaturated with sugar. In either case, it was believed that evil influences were responsible for the failure of the syrup to caramelize. To counteract the evil influences and prevent failure, the cakes were made only during good weather and not on rainy days. While the rice cakes were being made, it was thought that the door had to be closed and no visitors would be admitted to the home. Children were not permitted in the kitchen. Pomelo leaves, placed in the water used to make the syrup, were believed to purify the water and dispel the evil influences.

During this time, the men of the household worked at general home repairs while the women kept busy sewing new window curtains, pillow cases, blanket covers and clothes.

On the twentieth day of the twelfth moon, house cleaning started. Every room was cleaned. Chests of drawers, cabinets, cupboards and shelves were cleaned and relined. The house was redecorated, the altar reconditioned, the furniture polished, the front gate painted, the windows cleaned and the walls washed.

After house cleaning, the pantry was stocked. Provisions and delicacies for the New Year such as ham, preserved duck, shark's fins, bird's nests, dried mushrooms, dried sea cucumber and dried oysters were purchased. Additional delicacies might include dried prawns, exotic teas, sweetmeats, melon seeds and oranges. The rice bin was replenished almost to the brim. A partially filled or empty bin on New Year's Day was considered an omen of a poor harvest and poverty.

Gifts of fine foods, rare teas, delicious fruits, live poultry, freshly made sweetmeats and cakes were exchanged between relatives and friends. Other gifts of expensive cloth, quality jewelry, flowering plants or bearing dwarfed fruit trees might also be exchanged. Cut flowers were not considered appropriate for the occasion.

The old "spring couplets" 春聯, written with gold ink on strips of red paper and posted the previous year, were removed and replaced with new ones on the gates, doors and halls. Year-old pictures of the Door Gods 門神 put on the doors to protect the home and its inhabitants were also removed and replaced. In the same spirit, delinquent accounts and debts were settled before the New Year.

On the twenty-fourth day of the twelfth moon, the Kitchen God 竈君 was honored and worshipped before he departed for Heaven to report to the Jade Emperor 玉皇 on the activities of the family during the past year. In addition to incense and candles, offerings of cakes, candy and sweetmeats were placed on the family altar. The Kitchen God's portrait, posted near the stove, was smeared with honey on the lips—a sort of bribe so that his report would be favorable. To send him off to Heaven, this picture was then removed from the kitchen and burned in the courtyard.

About a week before the New Year, the New Year puddings were made. Glutinous rice flour and syrup made with slabs of Chinese brown sugar were mixed and poured into pans lined with moistened bamboo leaves. The size of the puddings varied. Some were huge, measuring about twenty inches in diameter and eight inches in height and requiring about fourteen to sixteen hours of steaming time in a large wok 鑊 set on an outdoor stove fueled with wood. After the pudding was cooked, the bamboo leaves were trimmed. The dark brown pudding was decorated with dried red jujubes 紅棗 to symbolize "early good fortune" and white sesame seeds 芝蔴 to signify the gift of "many sons."

On the last day of the year (this day varied with different localities), the Kitchen God returned from Heaven and his new portrait was posted near the stove. That evening, ceremonies to "round out the year" 團年 were performed at the family altar, thanking Heaven and Earth, the household gods and the ancestors for the blessings received during the year.

Following the ceremonies, which were concluded with the burning of a packet of firecrackers, the family gathered for dinner.

New Year offerings: citrus fruits, blooming narcissus plant, box of sweetmeats, New Year pudding

After the meal, the table was cleared, dishes were washed and put away. Then it was time to undertake final preparations to greet the New Year. A new tablecloth was put on the dining table. New dishes and new chopsticks were brought out. The beds were made up with new sheets, new pillow cases and blanket covers. The sweetmeat and melon seed dishes were filled. Fragrant Chinese narcissus plants 水仙花 with only fresh blossoms and buds were purchased from vendors. The living room and altar were decorated with pomelos, oranges, tangerines, New Year puddings and blooming narcissus plants.

When the traditional vegetarian dish named *chai* 齋 was prepared, all preparations for greeting the New Year were completed.

New Year Celebration

Everyone, young and old, rich and poor, looked forward to celebrating the noisiest, most joyous and longest festival of the year. Chinese New Year was not celebrated at a hotel or supper club with revelers donning silly paper hats, drinking liquor and champagne, eating sumptuously, blowing whistles, twirling noisy rattles and throwing confetti while singing ''Auld Lang Syne'' and dancing until the wee hours of the morning. In China, New Year's Day was a solemn occasion. Every family performed religious rites at the family altar. This was the time for a family reunion. All family quarrels had been amiably settled and forgotten.

Between 11 p.m. and 1 a.m., the hour of the Rat, the entire family, dressed in new garments and robes, assembled at the newly decorated family altar. Outsiders were not included in this gathering, and each family performed its own rites. An individual without a family was a lonely soul indeed when it came time to greet the New Year.

The family elder lighted the incense and candles and performed the Triple Rites, beseeching Heaven and Earth, the household gods and the spirits of his ancestors to bestow blessings for the ensuing year. The ceremony was concluded with the burning of a long string of firecrackers.

Children were kept awake for the ceremony because it was believed that this custom ensured parental longevity. Following the ceremony, the family gathered for the first meal of the new year. This was traditionally a vegetarian meal made with vermicelli, fried bean curds, fermented bean curds, bean curd sticks, rice flour sticks, ginkgo nuts, lotus seeds, dried lily buds and dried scales of the lily bulbs. Other ingredients included algae, snow peas, dried fungi, dried mushrooms and chestnuts. Lettuce, *sheng tsai* 生菜, was served with the meal because it is a close homonym of the word for prosperity, *sheng tsai* 生財. Everyone was required to have a second serving of rice to symbolize plentiful food in the coming year.

After the meal, when the table had been cleared and the dishes washed, tea with sweetmeats were served to the parents. The serving was performed according to the prescribed rank of the family, beginning with the oldest son. Tea was served and received with both hands. After one or two sips, more tea was added. Parents showed their appreciation by extending New Year's greetings and presenting gifts of money wrapped in red paper 封包. This ceremony demonstrated filial piety, the cardinal virtue.

In the morning, people dressed in their new

clothes and shoes. Men, without their wives, called on relatives and friends to wish them a "Happy and Prosperous New Year" 恭喜發財. The caller was served tea with sweetmeats; melon seeds, both red and black; and fruits and delicacies such as puffed rice cakes, dumplings and deep-fried round doughnuts. In addition, liquor and tobacco were offered. Before leaving, the well-wisher presented gifts of money wrapped in red paper to all the unmarried children of the family.

For the first five days of the year, men alone made the visits. This would appear chauvinistic by today's standards but was actually very practical. Since each family was keeping open-house, the wife and children remained at home to receive visitors. However, after the fifth day, women made visits either alone or accompanied by their husbands. When women went on New Year visits, they always took a gift, usually a sack of oranges.

Certain things had to be avoided on New Year's Day. The lights on the porch and in the parlor were not turned off but left on continuously. To retain good fortune and wealth in the home, the house was not swept for fear of sweeping out the good fortune. No knife was used, even to prepare meals. Quarrels were to be avoided. Words with bad connotations such as defeat, illness, surgical operations, a coffin or death were not to be used. Dishes were handled carefully, for breaking a dish on New Year's Day indicated bad luck for the coming year.

The first ten days of the New Year were dedicated to the various components of a proper household. Although no special ceremonies were performed for the dedicatees except on the seventh day, the day for mankind 人日, one had to be careful not to kill a fowl or animal for food on the day dedicated to it. On the seventh day, everyone became one year older.

	Day
1	Chicken
2	Dog
3	Pig
4	Duck
5	Cattle
6	Horse
7	Mankind
8	Rice and certain cereals
9	Fruits and vegetables
10	Wheat and barley

Traditionally, meat was not served on New Year's day. People ate only vegetarian meals.

The second day was a day of feasting 開年. Abstinence from meat was over, and all types of exotic food were permitted. The New Year pudding was cut and served. The evening meal might include chicken, fresh pork, preserved pork products, preserved duck and other delicacies.

On the third day, sacrifice was made to the God of Wealth 財神. Shops and businesses rarely opened before the third day. Most remained closed for at least five days.

On the fourth day, the bath houses in old China reopened.

On the seventh day, dedicated to mankind, sumptuous feasting resumed. If there was another New Year pudding still intact and on display, it was cut and eaten on this day.

The New Year celebration lasted for fifteen days, allowing time for various entertainments to be enjoyed, including games of mah-jong and dominos at home or at clubs. There were also animal shows featuring trained dogs and monkeys, theatrical plays staged by amateur and professional troupes, acrobatic performances, magic shows, puppet shows, storytelling and lion and dragon dances.

Lantern Festival

The Lantern Festival 燈節 was celebrated on the fifteenth day of the first moon to mark the conclusion of the New Year festivities. This festival originated about two thousand years ago during the Han 漢 dynasty as a way of assuring continued prosperity and longevity. Large red lanterns illuminated with candles were placed at the door and also used to decorate the trees and garden. In the evening, people of both sexes paraded through the streets and alleys carrying lanterns of various sizes and shapes—a most colorful display.

In some villages, it was customary for members of the clan to dine together in the ancestral hall on the evening of the Lantern Festival. A tree limb with many branches was used as a decorative device suggesting the clan's continued branching.

Birthday of the Local Earth God

The birthday of the local Earth God 土地誕 was usually celebrated on the second day of the second moon, although this date varied in different localities. People burned incense, candles and paper offerings and prayed at the shrine of the local Earth God.

The worshipping of the spirit of the earth or land, a primitive animistic practice, antedated other religious practices in China. It was based on the belief that all things whether animate or inanimate possessed a spirit or soul. There

were many earth gods, each with a specific jurisdiction. The Duke or God of the Earth 社公 had a large jurisdiction which might include an entire district or province. The authority of a God of the Walled City 城隍 extended over an entire city. By comparison, the local Earth God 土地 administered a very limited area, such as that of a home, a field or a village.

The local Earth God, accepted by both Taoists and Buddhists, served as the local registrar for births, marriages and death. He was extremely close to the people and involved with their personal problems. People prayed to him for help in healing the sick and solving ordinary difficulties. He was considered a personal protector because the people knew him intimately. In many ways, the local Earth God was even more popular than Kuan Yin 觀音, the Goddess of Mercy.

Anyone might be declared a local Earth God after death, especially a person who had performed outstanding or meritorious service in the community. By the same token, a local Earth God who did not fulfill or discharge his duties faithfully could be relieved from his post and be replaced.

The unpretentious shrine of the local Earth God was seen in every city, in the temple grounds, along the roadsides and beside the banks of rivers. He was represented by a small idol in a sitting position or by a pointed stone, fronted by a trough or receptacle used for the burning of incense and candles.

Since the Ming 明 dynasty, the image of the local Earth God has been set on the ground and not housed in the main temple. According to legend, Emperor Tai Tsu 太祖, who reigned from 1368 to 1399, stopped at an inn for dinner on one of his trips. All the tables were occupied with guests except one, which had an idol of the local Earth God set upon it. The emperor commanded that the idol be removed from the table and set on the ground outside so that he could use the table. Later the innkeeper set the idol back on the table. But in a dream, the local Earth God appeared to the innkeeper. He did not want to violate the emperor's command and insisted that he be put back on the ground outside the inn.

Birthday of the Goddess of Mercy

The birthday of the Goddess of Mercy or Bodhisattva Kuan Yin 觀音菩薩誕 was cele-brated on the nineteenth day of the second moon. This festival, held at the temple and at the family altar, consisted of burning incense, candles and paper offerings, and praying and abstaining from meat for the entire day. The faithful honored her with similar rites on the first and fifteenth day of every moon. In addi-tion, she was worshipped on the nineteenth day of the sixth moon, which was considered to be the anniversary of the day she started her holy life, and on the nineteenth day of the ninth moon, which was the anniversary of the day of her enlightenment.

Buddhism, introduced in China in the first century A.D., brought new concepts of conduct and of life after death to the Chinese. In Buddhism, nirvana is the state of perfect bless-edness. To a certain degree, it is similar to the Western idea of Heaven as the dwelling place of God, angels and souls who have achieved salvation, but for Buddhists nirvana primarily signifies release from the cycle of reincarna-tion. A Bodhisattva or Pusa 菩薩 is an ad-vanced soul who vows, out of compassion, not to enter the final state of nirvana until there are no others remaining behind who can be helped toward that goal.

When introduced into China by Buddhist missionaries from India, the Bodhisattva of Compassion was Avalokitesvara, depicted as a stout man with whiskers. In China, this deity acquired a new name and, over the course of centuries, changed from male to female. Kuan Yin, or "She Who Looks Down and Hears the Cries of the World," became one of the most popular deities in the Chinese pantheon. Buddhists and Taoists accepted and adored her. She was loved while other deities were feared. Women confided in her, poured out their troubles and sought comfort from her. Men prayed and sought blessings from her in time of need. She symbolized love, tenderness, pity and forgiveness.

Pictures and images depicted the Goddess of Mercy in many forms, attesting to her powers to do many things. She was sometimes seen as a goddess dressed in splendid robes; other times she was seen carrying a child or holding the "vase of Immortality," or holding a willow bough. She was often depicted standing on a rock in the midst of a turbulent sea protecting a troubled mariner, or as a figure with many arms.

The first legend about the Goddess of Mercy was written down during the Sung 宋 dynasty by a Buddhist monk. He wrote that long ago, there lived a cruel and ruthless king named Miao Chuang Wang 妙莊王, whose kingdom was situated somewhere east of Burma and south of Thailand. This country was possibly in the area of present-day Cambodia.

The king was sad because he did not have any children, especially a son to succeed him on the throne. The king and queen made a pil-

Goddess of Mercy (17th century)

and chose instead to devote her life to prayer and meditation.

Miao Shan's decision angered the king. She was confined to quarters in the garden court of the palace. But the queen beseeched the king and he finally relented. Miao Shan was allowed to enter the White Sparrow Convent as a novice. The king commanded the abbess of the convent to make life miserable for his daughter, but Miao Shan was not discouraged by these hardships, even when assigned to perform demeaning tasks. All the animals helped her. Birds brought her vegetables, the sea-dragon dug a well for her near her kitchen and tigers gathered firewood.

When he realized that his ploy had failed to change her mind, the king dispatched soldiers to burn the convent. Miao Shan pricked the roof of her mouth with a sliver of bamboo and spat blood which immediately changed to rain and extinguished the flames. Executioners were dispatched to behead her. When the sword was raised, the blade was broken into a thousand pieces.

Eventually Miao Shan committed suicide by strangling herself with a bow string rather than incur the relentless wrath of her father. She then descended into hell 地獄. There, with piety and prayer, she released the lost souls and converted hell into a paradise. Yen-Lo Wang 閻羅王, the Ruler of Hell, petitioned the Jade Emperor 玉皇 to have her expelled from hell. She was transported back to earth on a lotus flower and lived on the island of Pootoo 普陀, near present-day Shanghai. Here, for nine years, she prayed, meditated, administered to the sick, cured illnesses and rescued shipwrecked sailors.

By divine revelation, Miao Shan discovered that the Jade Emperor had directed the God of

grimage to the shrine of the Celestial Ruler, confessed their sins and prayed for children. Subsequently, they were blessed with three daughters but no sons. The oldest was named Miao Yu 妙欲, the second was Miao Yin 妙音 and the youngest was called Miao Shan 妙善. She was born on the nineteenth day of the second moon.

When his daughters became eligible for marriage, the king, anxious to have a male heir to succeed him, set out to find suitable husbands for them. The two oldest daughters obeyed their father and were married. But Miao Shan refused to obey her father, renounced marriage

Epidemics to punish her father for his sins. He was afflicted with open sores which were incurable except with medication compounded from the hands and eyes of the living. Miao Shan disguised herself as a priest-physician and visited her ailing father. After examining the strange and puzzling malady, she advised her father that medicine made from the hands and eyes of the living was the only cure. Since no one could be found who was willing to part with the needed ingredients, she told the king to send an emissary to Pootoo, where he would find them.

When a minister arrived at Pootoo, Miao Shan told him to chop off her hands, gouge out her eyes and place them on a golden platter for presentation to the king. This was done, the medicine was prepared and the king was cured of his disease.

But when the queen saw the scar on the severed hand, she realized that the hands and eyes were those of Miao Shan. The king and queen journeyed to Pootoo to thank their daughter and repent. Arriving at the temple, they discovered Miao Shan sitting on the altar with blood dripping from her amputated limbs and eyeless sockets. They begged forgiveness, repented and prayed for their daughter to be made whole again. Immediately her hands and eyes were restored. The king mended his ways, and he and the queen became devout Buddhists.

To honor his dutiful daughter, the king commissioned a sculptor to make a statue of Miao Shan "complete with hands and complete with eyes," *chuan shou chuan yen* 全手全眼. The sculptor thought he had said "a thousand hands and a thousand eyes," *chien shou chien yen* 千手千眼, and made his statue accordingly. Thereafter the Goddess of Mercy was often depicted with many arms.

Clear and Bright Festival

People in many cultures have welcomed and celebrated the reawakening of nature in the spring. As trees sprout tender buds and leaves, the days of snow and bitter cold are finally left behind. Insects, birds and animals reappear, and people replace thick heavy clothing with thin light garments. In China the days were now clear and bright, a time for rejoicing.

The date of Ching Ming 清明, the Clear and Bright Festival, was based on the position of the sun, unlike that of the Christian spring festival, Easter, which is based on the cycles of the moon. Ching Ming was usually held 15 days after the spring equinox, or 104 days after the winter solstice, a date corresponding to April 5 on our calendar.

In ancient China, youths wore garlands on their heads and danced along the river banks and in the meadows to celebrate the coming of spring. Later the celebration became the Tree Planting Festival or Arbor Day 植樹節, when the emperor or his delegate participated in a ritual planting of trees in the palace grounds. Eventually the nature of the festival changed again, becoming the Clear and Bright Festival, the first of the three festivals for the dead.

Chinese Taoists believed that man possessed many types of souls—three types of spirit souls 魂 and seven types of animal souls 魄. After death, a spirit soul proceeded to hell 地獄 for judgment, punishment and reincarnation. An animal soul hovered around the corpse and the grave. Another spirit soul resided at the ancestral tablet. The spirits of the dead were thought to have mundane needs such as food, clothing and money in the world beyond. It was the duty of the descendants to provide for these needs by offering sacrifices periodically at the grave. Ancestors adequately provided for were benevolent. Their spirits provided rainfall for the crops and insured bountiful harvests. They also maintained the continued well-being and prosperity of their descendants. Neglected and hungry ancestors were malevolent. Their spirits caused all kinds of misfortunes for their descendants.

To celebrate the Clear and Bright Festival, an auspicious day for making sacrifices and honoring ancestors was selected during a month-long period from April 5 to May 4. Families worshipped at the family grave while the clan worshipped at the clan's oldest ancestral grave. The rite of worshipping at the grave 拜山 or "sweeping the tomb" 掃墓 was performed in the morning. It was believed that the ancestral spirits were able to spend the entire day with their descendants before returning to the graves at sundown.

To prepare for the ritual, overgrown grass at the grave was cut, weeds were removed and the tomb was repaired and decorated. A temporary altar was set up on the ground in front of the grave. In old China artificial flowers were used to decorate the grave, since fresh flowers were not considered appropriate for that purpose. The one exception was the willow, symbolizing light and vitality and thus an enemy of darkness.

The use of the willow began during the time of Emperor Kao Tsung 高宗 of the Tang 唐 dynasty, who reigned from 650 to 683. He commanded his subordinates to adorn their caps with willow branches to ward off evil spirits. Later the willow began to be used during the Clear and Bright Festival to decorate graves and provide protection from evil spirits. Women adorned their hair with willow, hung willow amulets around their necks and carried

willow charms in their pockets or pinned them on their clothing. Since the willow was used for grave decoration, the Chinese were reluctant to plant willow around their homes. Another tree not planted around the home was the mulberry, because in Chinese the words for mulberry, *sang* 桑, and funeral or mourning, *sang* 喪, are homonyms.

Next to the altar, on a low stand, five place settings were prepared with tea, wine and rice with chopsticks. Various foods were offered, either simple or elaborate depending on the affluence of the family. There were usually five

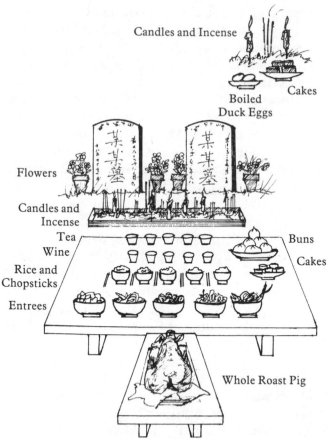

Grave offerings for the Clear and Bright Festival

dishes, which could be chicken, fish, shrimp, *tou fu*, oysters, pork, boiled duck eggs or buns. A whole roast pig was considered the richest food offering. In addition, three sticks of burning incense and a few simple dishes such as peanuts, cookies, fruits, boiled duck eggs, pork or chicken were set on the ground a short distance to the left of the grave. These were for the stray ghosts and hungry spirits roaming around the hill and graves. If any hungry spirits stopped by, they would eat this food and not bother the dishes prepared for an ancestor.

Family members, according to rank and seniority, burned incense and candles, bowed, prayed and made offerings of tea, wine and food. Then paper offerings—gold and silver paper folded to represent bullion and paper money for use in hell—were burned. This ceremony honored the ancestors and assured that they would be adequately supplied with food and money for the ensuing year. The burning of a packet of firecrackers concluded the ceremony. Families then picnicked at the cemetery or gathered at a restaurant for a luncheon following these rites.

In the People's Republic of China, the old ceremonies associated with the burial of the dead and the Clear and Bright Festival have not been honored. In old China the fields used to be dotted with graves and the hills pocketed with tombs. Today these graves have been exhumed and the grave sites on arable land have been converted into fields for planting. Those on hillsides not considered suitable for agriculture have been planted with trees. Concrete tombs and tombstones have even been broken and the material used for road construction.

The new government officially advocates cremation of the dead to conserve much-needed arable land. The late Premier Chou En-Lai 周恩來 was cremated and his ashes were strewn over the hills, valleys and rivers of China.

Today the Clear and Bright Festival held on April 5 in the People's Republic of China is not a festival to honor and worship the spirits of the ancestors. It is instead a celebration to honor the departed revolutionary heroes of modern China. The term "Spring Festival" is now used to designate the lunar New Year.

Birthday of Buddha

The most important Buddhist celebration was the birthday of Buddha 佛誕, held on the eighth day of the fourth moon. This celebration honored Gautama or Sakyamuni Buddha 釋迦牟尼佛 with the burning of incense, candles and paper offerings, and with prayers and abstention from eating meat.

Although there have been many Buddhas, some mythical and some real, some before and some after Sakyamuni Buddha, the history of Buddhism began with Sakyamuni. He is considered the principal Buddha, the true Buddha, the historical Buddha and the founder of the Buddhist religion.

Prince Siddharta, sage of the royal house of Sakya, was born in 624 B.C. at Kapilavastu on the Indian side of the Himalayas, in present-day Nepal. His Brahman father was King Suddhodhana. His mother, also of royal blood, was Queen Maya. According to legend, Queen Maya conceived miraculously after she dreamt of her son coming from Heaven. The prince was born from her side after she had a vision of a many-tusked white elephant.

At birth, the god Indra, a male deity, appeared as an old woman to assist with the delivery. Brahma and the other gods appeared to greet the new baby. All nature rejoiced. Cool breezes stirred the trees and the trees burst into bloom. Springs welled up from the ground. Great light illuminated the earth and saints presented flowers. Immediately after his birth, the prince took seven steps to the east and seven steps to the west. Four mighty dragons appeared and poured water from Heaven for the infant's baptism.

As an adult, the prince had a large skull, broad forehead, dark eyes and forty teeth that were even and white. His skin had a fine texture without blemishes and was the color of gold. He had three lucky lines on his neck, earlobes that were split and elongated and eyebrows that were joined together. His legs were like those of a gazelle. There was also a mark at the center of his forehead symbolizing the third eye of wisdom.

A fortune teller predicted that if he remained at home, he would become a mighty ruler and all nations would bow to him. Such a ruler appeared only once in ten thousand years. However, if he renounced worldly life and wandered away from home, he would become a great saint and a teacher of mankind. Mindful of the predictions, the king showered his son with all manner of luxuries. He wanted the prince to be happy and content at all times so that he would remain at home. The young Siddharta was carefully guarded from sad and unpleasant experiences.

Nevertheless, one day while riding outside the palace in his gilded chariot drawn by a team of white horses, he observed poverty, misery, pain and death. He saw a poor man dressed in tattered rags begging for food and alms. He encountered a sick man lying on the roadside writhing in pain. He saw a corpse followed by people weeping and wailing. These experiences sealed his destiny. Eventually he met a monk who was begging for food. The monk, in spite of his poverty, appeared happy and at peace. After a discussion with the monk, the prince decided to give up all his earthly possessions in order to find peace and wisdom, so that he could then teach mankind how to overcome the miseries of life.

That night when everyone was asleep in the palace, he renounced his wealth, power and high position and quietly bade good-bye to his wife and infant son. Although he wished earnestly to embrace his son for the last time, he controlled his emotions and left without doing so. His servant and his favorite horse, Khantaka, were waiting for him. As he left the palace, gods strewed flowers on the road to deaden the sounds of his horse's hooves and the city gates opened miraculously to permit his departure.

He traveled all night and dismounted at daybreak. He took off his royal robes and replaced them with the tattered clothes of a beggar. He removed all his jewelry and instructed his servant to return them to his father. He cut off his hair and beard with his sword. His horse, with great respect and reverence, kissed his feet. He told his servant to return with his horse to the palace.

For the next six years, he wandered as a homeless ascetic seeking the truth. He begged for his food and drank water from melted snow. But the truth eluded him.

Finally he secluded himself in the jungle at Uruvela, where he sat in meditation under a fig tree called the pipal or Bo tree. He made a solemn vow that he would not leave that spot until he had found the truth. Although spirits from hell attempted to scare him off with threats of bodily harm, their weapons fell like lotus petals. Mara, the Evil One, tempted him by sending his three beautiful daughters named Desire, Pleasure and Delight to stir and excite his passions. But in his presence the three maidens were transformed into ugly witches. Mara was defeated. All the spirits in Heaven rejoiced at his victory over passion.

One day, he looked up from his meditation and saw the morning star glimmering in the heavens. At that moment, like a prisoner confined in a dark dungeon who is suddenly exposed to bright light, he found the truth and was greatly enlightened. He was thirty-five years old when he attained Buddhahood.

He delivered his first sermon, on the "Turning of the Wheel," in Deer Park near Benares. Unlike the Brahmans who preached only to the privileged caste, the Buddha delivered his sermons to all people—rich and poor, young and old, men and women. Soon his disciples dispersed in every direction spreading his teachings. Even when he was old and infirm, he continued to travel from village to village teaching the truth.

He died at the age of eighty and was cremated at Kusinara, about 120 miles from Benares. His relics were divided among eight kings who built temples and stupas to enshrine them. Some of these relics were later carried to China. Eventually Buddhism spread far and wide, to China, Korea, Japan, Syria, Sri Lanka and all the countries of Southeast Asia.

According to a Chinese monk who lived toward the end of the Han 漢 dynasty, around A.D. 200, Buddhism was introduced into China during the reign of Ming Ti 明帝, who ruled from A.D. 58 to 76. Legend has it that the emperor dreamt he saw a bright light. A seer who interpreted the dream predicted that two In-

Seated Buddha (T'ang period)

dian monks riding white horses would arrive in China carrying Buddhist books and sutras.

The White Horse Monastery 白馬寺 in the city of Loyang 洛陽 was the first Buddhist monastery built in China. It was constructed around A.D. 60 to house two Indian monks who had come riding on white horses to teach Buddhism. The monastery was rebuilt and restored many times in the following centuries. The present buildings date from the Ming 明 dynasty (1368-1644) and were most recently restored in 1957. In front of the main entrance are two large white stone horses. There are also two grave mounds in the courtyard near the entrance where the two Indian monks are said to be buried.

The fundamental teachings of the Buddha are contained in the Four Noble Truths:

1. Life is suffering.
2. The cause of suffering is desire.
3. The end of suffering is freedom from desire.
4. There is a path leading to the end of suffering.

The Buddhist path leading to the end of suffering is called the Eightfold Path, and it prescribes a way of living according to right ideas, right feelings, right speech, right actions, right livelihood, right obedience, right mindfulness and right meditation.

Fifth Moon Festival

The second festival for the living, commonly called the Fifth Moon Festival 五月節, was celebrated on the fifth day of the fifth moon. The proper name for this festival was the Upright Sun Festival 端陽節, but foreigners in China referred to it as the Dragon-boat Festival 龍船節.

During the fifth moon, which includes the summer solstice, the weather in China is hot and humid. People were uncomfortable in the muggy atmosphere. Snakes, lizards, toads, centipedes, scorpions, spiders and other insects appeared in great numbers. Children developed sores on their bodies, and infections and parasitic diseases were common. Therefore the fifth moon, also called the evil, wicked or pestilential moon, was fraught with anxiety.

Prevention of Disease

On the fifth day of the fifth moon, people throughout China brought out their amulets, charms and aromatic leaves in the belief that these talismans could protect individuals and places from demons and evil spirits that were responsible for causing diseases. A branch of mugwort 艾草, a spray of willow or the sword-like calamus leaves 菖蒲 were put up at the sides of gates or hung over the doors. People carried mugwort, scallions, garlic, pomelo leaves and pomegranate leaves, or sachets containing incense, aromatic leaves or substances such as camphor balls and charms. These were fastened on women's hair, carried in the pockets, hung on clothes buttons or pinned on clothing.

A charm with magic words written on yellow paper and depicting the "five poisonous creatures" 五毒 was considered extremely effective for counteracting harmful influences. The five poisonous creatures were the snake or lizard, centipede, scorpion, spider and the toad.

The snake was thought to be a ghost which could assume the form of a man to induce girls to marry him, or assume the guise of a beautiful woman who seduced men. The Chinese were deathly afraid of lizards. They were extremely careful to make sure that the salt jar was covered, for it was believed that when a lizard crawled over food, especially salt, the food became poisonous. They were afraid that if the tail of a lizard separated from the body and somehow wiggled into the external canal of one's ear, deafness would result. Also, if a lizard crawled into the ear of a person who was sleeping, the lizard could suck out the person's brain. Centipedes, scorpions and spiders were feared because of the danger that they might sting the occupants of a home. The toad, an animal of the night, was thought to possess an invisible arrow which could inflict death by transmitting malaria.

On the fifth day of the fifth moon, the character for prince or sovereign, *wang* 王, was often written in vermilion on the foreheads of children. The three horizontal lines of the character were thought to represent the wrinkles on the forehead of a tiger. The character for tiger, *fu* 虎, could be written instead of *wang* on the child's forehead or on both cheeks. It was believed that the tiger, the most ferocious indigenous wild animal in China, was able to dispel demons and evil spirits.

For further protection against malignant influences, some people drank a concoction of sulfur 硫磺 and cinnabar 硃砂 dissolved in wine. The leftover solution was smeared on children's nose, ears and face to prevent pimples and skin ulcers. The solution was also sprinkled throughout the home to protect it against evil influences, vermin and the five poisonous creatures. Others attempted to purify the home by fumigating it with the fumes of burning sulfur or by simply sprinkling it with vinegar.

Dragon-boat Races

The Fifth Moon Festival was also noted for its dragon-boat races, especially in the southern provinces, where there are many rivers and lakes. This regatta commemorated the death of Chu Yuan 屈原, an honest minister who is said to have committed suicide by drowning himself in a river.

Chu Yuan was a minister in the kingdom of Chu 楚, situated in present-day Hunan 湖南 and Hupeh 湖北 provinces, during the Warring States 戰國 period (475–221 B.C.). He was upright, loyal and highly esteemed for his wise counsel that had brought peace and prosperity to the kingdom. However, when a dishonest and corrupt prince vilified Chu Yuan, he was disgraced and dismissed from his office. Realizing that the country was now in the hands of evil and corrupt officials, Chu Yuan clasped a large stone and leaped into the Mi Lo 汨羅 river on the fifth day of the fifth moon. Nearby fishermen rushed over and tried to save him, but they were unable even to recover his body. Thereafter, the kingdom declined and was eventually conquered by the kingdom of Chin 秦.

The people of Chu, mourning the death of Chu Yuan, threw rice into the river to feed his hungry ghost every year on the fifth day of the fifth moon. One year, the spirit of Chu Yuan appeared and told the mourners that a huge reptile in the river had stolen the rice that had been offered. The spirit advised them to wrap

Charm depicting the Five Poisonous Creatures

the rice in silk and bind it with five different colored threads before tossing it into the river.

On the Fifth Moon Festival, a glutinous rice pudding called *tsung* 粽 was eaten to symbolize the rice offerings to Chu Yuan. Ingredients such as beans, lotus seeds, chestnuts, pork fat and the golden yolk of a salted duck egg were often added to the glutinous rice. The pudding was wrapped with bamboo leaves, bound with a sort of raffia and boiled in salt water for hours.

The dragon-boat races represented the attempts to rescue and recover the body of Chu Yuan. A dragon-boat ranged from fifty to one hundred feet in length with a beam of about five and a half feet, accommodating two paddlers sitting side by side. A wooden dragon head was attached at the bow, and a dragon tail at the stern. A banner hoisted on a pole was also fastened at the stern. The hull was decorated with a design of red, green and blue scales edged in gold. In the center of the boat was a canopied shrine. Behind the shrine sat drummers, gong-beaters and cymbal-crashers who would set the pace for the paddlers. Men standing at the bow set off firecrackers, tossed rice into the water and made believe they were looking for Chu Yuan. All the noise and pageantry created an atmosphere of gaiety and excitement for the participants and spectators. Competitions were held between different clans, villages and organizations, and winners were awarded medals, banners, jugs of wine and festive meals.

After the races, the wooden head and tail of the dragon were detached and stored either at the clan headquarters or at the local temple. The hull was buried in the muddy river to prevent cracking, warping and shrinkage. The boats were therefore reconditioned annually before the festival.

Some people believed that the purpose of the dragon-boat races was not to commemorate the death of Chu Yuan, who was a relatively insignificant minister, but to placate the hungry ghosts of people who had drowned. Others believed the races were held to propitiate the dragons who lived in the rivers and lakes. As the dispenser of rain and water, the dragon had to be appeased to insure an adequate supply for the farmers in the coming hot months of summer.

As with the lunar New Year and Mid-

Minister Chu Yuan

Autumn festivals, delinquent accounts were settled before the festivities. The Fifth Moon Festival was also celebrated in the home with a brief ceremony at the family altar. Incense, candles and paper offerings were burned and prayers said. An offering of the special *tsung* was included. The ceremony concluded with the burning of a packet of firecrackers, followed by a lavish family feast.

Birthday of the God of War

The Birthday of the God of War, Kuan Ti 關帝, was usually celebrated at temples dedicated to him on the thirteenth day of the fifth moon. Kuan Ti was a famous warrior who lived in the second and third centuries.

The story of Kuan Ti takes us through some interesting history. The first emperor of China, Chin Shih Huang Ti 秦始皇帝, unified the country by subduing the many independent feudal states and bringing them together under one empire. His reign was very short, lasting from 221 to 206 B.C. The Han 漢 dynasty which followed flourished for more than four centuries, from 206 B.C. to A.D. 220. The Chinese looked back to this dynasty with great pride. The country was at peace and well ruled; it prospered and expanded. But like all great empires, the Han dynasty eventually decayed and disintegrated. At the end, incompetent emperors were enthroned. Some were infants, some were in their teens and one was a feeble-minded imbecile. Power was concentrated in the hands of court eunuchs, and corrupt officials finally usurped the throne. When the dynasty finally ended, the country was divided into the Three Kingdoms 三國.

This division occurred when the unscrupulous Tsao Tsao 曹操, an adopted son of a court eunuch, persuaded the last emperor of the Han to abdicate. Tsao Tsao then seized the north and northwestern parts of the empire and established the kingdom of Wei 魏. At approximately the same time, Sun Chuan 孫權, a general who was the son of an official, occupied the south and southeast and declared himself emperor of the kingdom of Wu 吳. Descendants of the imperial family named Liu 劉 took over the west and southwest. Liu Pei 劉備 became the founding emperor of the kingdom of Shu 蜀.

The *Romance of the Three Kingdoms* 三國志演義, written in the late 1300s, is composed of many adventurous tales set during that time. Episodes from this famous novel have been retold by storytellers for centuries and have served as themes for poems, plays and operas. Loyalty, intrigue, magic, military battles, wickedness and corruption are all contained in the *Romance of the Three Kingdoms*, and in it are to be found the stories of heroes such as Liu Pei, Chang Fei 張飛 and Kuan Yu 關羽.

According to legend, Liu Pei, although of royal blood, was a seller of straw sandals and baskets. He was about eight feet tall, and he had long ears with lobes extending to his shoulders. His eyes protruded to such an extent that it was possible for him to see backwards behind his ears. His gawky hands hung down below his knees. His complexion, however, was jade-like.

Chang Fei was a butcher and a seller of wine. He was also about eight feet tall. His head was bullet-shaped like that of a leopard. His eyes were large. His chin was pointed like a swallow and his deep voice resembled thunder.

Kuan Yu was probably born in the present-day province of Shansi 山西 around A.D. 162 and lived to the year 220. Although his given name was Chang Sheng 長生, he was also known as Shou Chang 壽長 and Yun Chang 雲長. He was a seller of bean curds who devoted himself to the pursuit of knowledge. After killing a magistrate who had forced the daughter of an aged couple to be his concubine, Shou Chang became a fugitive and fled to the neighboring province of Shensi 陝西. While crossing a mountain pass, or *kuan* 關, he saw his reflection in a brook and noticed that his face had changed completely. At the border, he told the frontier guards that his name was Kuan Yu 關羽, "Pass of the Yu Family," and made good his escape.

In Chihli 直隸, situated in the present-day province of Hopei 河北, Liu Pei and Chang Fei were sitting in an inn drinking wine and formulating plans to defeat the rebels and restore peace to their troubled country. Kuan Yu, pushing a hand-cart, stopped at the inn for a rest and some wine to refresh himself. He turned to the waiter and said, "Be quick about it, for I am in haste to get into town and offer myself to the army."

Liu Pei and Chang Fei overheard the stranger and turned to look. They saw that he had a dark complexion, a huge body, a long beard and red lips. His eyes resembled those of a phoenix. His eyebrows looked like silkworms. He was awesome and dignified. It was said that Kuan had unusual strength and was indeed brave enough to stroke the beard of a tiger.

Liu Pei and Chang Fei introduced themselves to Kuan. The three joined together and continued to discuss how to save the country. At length, they decided to make a solemn oath of brotherhood at Chang Fei's peach orchard. With incense and candles burning at an altar under a blooming peach tree, they sacrificed a black ox and a white horse. With libations, they recited the following oath: "We three, Liu Pei, Kuan Yu and Chang Fei, though of different families, swear brotherhood and promise mutual help. We will rescue each other in difficulty; we will aid each other in danger. We ask not the same day of birth but we seek to die together. May Heaven the all-ruling and Earth the all-producing read our hearts, and if we ever turn aside from righteousness and forget kindliness, may Heaven and man strike us down."

After the oath, they bowed to each other. Liu Pei was the oldest and Chang Fei the youngest of the three sworn brothers. The black ox was prepared and a feast was held for the entire village.

For weapons, Liu Pei forged a double sword, Kuan Yu made a long-handled curved sword 關刀 weighing one hundred pounds and Chang Fei fashioned an eighteen-foot spear for himself. Each had a helmet and a full suit of armor.

The three sworn brothers remained loyal and faithful to their oath taken in the peach orchard. After Kuan Yu was captured and executed by Sun Chuan, Liu Pei died of grief, leaving his throne to his young son. Chang Fei wept tears of blood following Kuan Yu's execution and was subsequently assassinated.

Of the three sworn brothers, Kuan Yu was the only one who was later deified. During the Sung dynasty, he was elevated to Duke Kuan 關公. Then, during the reign of Emperor Wan Li 萬歷 (1573-1620) of the Ming dynasty, Duke Kuan was awarded the title "Supporter of Heaven and Protector of the Kingdom" and became "Kuan, the Supreme Ruler of the Universe" or Kuan Ti, the God of War 關帝.

The God of War was very popular through-

God of War

Republic of China adopted the God of War as their patron. In 1916, Yuan Shih-Kai 袁世凱, a warlord attempting to reinstate the monarchy with himself as emperor, decreed that both the God of War and Yo Fei 岳飛, a military hero of the Sung dynasty, be worshipped.

Many titles besides that of the God of War were conferred on Kuan Ti. Bean curd sellers adopted him as their patron, and he was considered a secondary God of Wealth. He was considered a God of Literature because it was claimed that he was able to recite from beginning to end "Tso's Commentary on the Spring and Autumn Annals" 春秋左傳. It was also believed that when he sharpened his sword, rain fell continuously for twenty-four hours. Thus he was considered a God of Rain. People also prayed to him as a God of Medicine because he was able to cure diseases caused by evil spirits.

Old-fashioned Chinese honored the Peach Orchard Oath to such an extent that marriages involving the surnames of Liu, Kuan and Chang were forbidden, because by oath the three heroes were blood relatives.

Worship of the Seven Sisters

In the evening of the seventh day of the seventh moon, women and maidens worshipped the Seven Sisters 拜七姐. This festival was also known as the Cowherd and the Weaver-Maid 牛郎織女 or simply the Seventh of the Seventh Moon 七月七.

A popular legend about the seven daughters of the Kitchen God has it that the prettiest of the daughters was the weaver-maid. She was attentive and industrious in her weaving of cloud-silk for the gods. Now, there was a young man in the country whose oldest brother

out China, and many temples were dedicated to him. Most revered in the Ching 清 dynasty (1644-1911), he was patron to the Ching emperors. It was said that the God of War helped the Ching Imperial Army defeat the White Lotus rebels in 1813, and in 1864 the God of War appeared in Heaven as the leader of an army that helped to defeat the Taiping Rebellion 太平仗.

After the revolution in 1911, soldiers of the

had an ill-tempered wife. One day this woman gave the young cowherd her husband's ox and drove him off the family farm. As it turned out, the ox had magical powers and gave good advice to his new master, who succeeded in all his endeavors and became exceedingly wealthy. When it came time for the cowherd to find a wife, the magic ox led his master to the Bridge of Fair Maidens. Here, much to his surprise, he found the seven daughters of the Kitchen God bathing in the river and stole the red clothes belonging to the weaver-maid. Six of the sisters returned to Heaven but the weaver-maid remained on earth to search for her clothes. When she discovered that they were at the home of the cowherd, she went there to retrieve them. Naturally the cowherd and the weaver-maid fell in love, and married. The marriage was a complete success. In three years they were blessed with two lovely children, a boy and a girl.

However, in her life on earth the weaver-maid had neglected her work as weaver for the gods. Angered, the gods decreed that she must return to Heaven and henceforth would be allowed to visit her husband only one night each year. These annual visits continued until the death of the cowherd, who was then transformed into an immortal and assigned to the star Altair in the constellation Aquila. The weaver-maid became the star Vega in the constellation Lyra, and her two children became the two little stars near Vega. The Queen of Heaven 天后 then drew the Milky Way or the Silver River 銀河 with her hairpin, separating the Celestial Cowherd from the Heavenly Weaver-Maid. Although husband and wife were able to see each other across the night sky, they were allowed to meet only once a year on the evening of the seventh day of the seventh moon.

On that night, if the sky was clear, magpies 喜鵲 gathered at the Milky Way and, by spreading their wings, formed a bridge so that the Weaver-Maid could cross the Celestial River and be with her lover. If it happened to rain that night, the river overflowed and the bridge could not be formed. The lovers had to wait until the following year, and it was said that the raindrops falling from the sky were their tears.

Around midnight on the seventh day of the seventh moon, people drew water from their spring or well which they then exposed to the

Celestial Cowherd and Heavenly Weaver-Maid at the Milky Way

morning dew and sun. It was believed that this specially treated water 河溪水 did not spoil and had magical properties. Kept in a home, it helped to protect the home against fire. It could be used to prepare medicines, and if one washed one's face or body with it, it not only prevented pimples and blemishes but also helped to cure skin disorders. Similarly, on that day women left their soap and cosmetics out in the courtyard to expose them to the starlight and sunlight.

The seventh day of the seventh moon was an auspicious day for general housecleaning as well. Clothes were sunned in the courtyard, and books similarly exposed were thought to be protected from bookworms. In the evening, women gathered at the temple to worship not only the Weaver-Maid but all the sisters. Offerings at the altar included melons, bananas, pomelos and the fruit called dragon's eye or longan 龍眼. Other offerings might be toilet articles such as a comb, face powder, soap and the like, and a basin of water purified with pomelo leaves for the ritual bath of the lovers.

The Weaver-Maid was the patroness of women and of needlework. Women praying to her sought her help in embroidery and other needlework, and in making their marriages happy and fruitful. The greatest blessing was to have many children, especially sons.

Fourteenth Day of the Seventh Moon

The different names, dates and ceremonies for the second festival for the dead, celebrated around the middle of the seventh moon, have caused much confusion. Taoists simply called this festival the "Fourteenth of the Seventh Moon" 七月十四 and performed ceremonies on two consecutive days, the fourteenth and fifteenth. The first ceremony was for the ancestors, and the second for the hungry ghosts. Some families reversed the order of the ceremonies, while others combined them, observing them both on the fourteenth.

Taoists and Buddhists believed that the souls of the dead imprisoned in hell were freed during the seventh month. From the last night of the sixth moon, when the gates of hell were opened, through the last night of the seventh moon, when they were closed again, the released souls were permitted to enjoy the feasts prepared for them. Taoists also believed that the spirits of the dead, most active at night, were capable of assuming different forms, appearing as snakes, moths, birds, foxes, wolves, tigers and so on. They were also able to appear as beautiful men or women in order to seduce the living. When they possessed an individual by entering the body, they caused illness and mental disorders. Ancestral spirits that were well fed and well cared for were benevolent and brought good fortune. Hungry ghosts with no descendants or those who were neglected were malevolent, causing droughts, floods and various misfortunes, including illness and death. Therefore it was essential for the ancestral spirits and the neglected hungry ghosts to be properly fed and cared for.

On the fourteenth day of the seventh moon, families worshipped their ancestors and provided their spirits with food and new clothes 拜家衣. Although it was not mandatory, some families visited their ancestral graves to cut any overgrown grass, remove weeds, repair the tombs and make offerings. Families that omitted the visit to the graves worshipped at the family altar with incense, candles, paper offerings and food. Colored paper representing cloth for clothing 衣紙 was burned. Smooth-finished paper represented silk while coarse paper stood for cotton cloth. Following the ceremony, the family gathered for a feast.

The next night, the same offerings were made for the hungry ghosts wandering in the streets and alleys 拜街衣. This ceremony was performed outside the front gate in the belief that doing so prevented the hungry ghosts from entering the courtyard and home.

Buddhists had a similar festival but referred to it as the Magnolia Festival 盂蘭盆會. It was observed from the fifteenth day to the end of the month. On these days, Buddhist priests 佛師 chanted and prayed for the dead.

Starting on the fifteenth day of the seventh moon, cake shops in China displayed moon cakes and candies in anticipation of the Mid-Autumn Festival just one month later.

Mid-Autumn Festival

The joyous Mid-Autumn Festival 中秋節, the third and last festival for the living, was celebrated on the fifteenth day of the eighth moon, around the time of the autumn equinox. Many referred to it simply as the "Fifteenth of the Eighth Moon" 八月十五. In the Western calendar, the day of the festival usually occurred sometime between the second week of September and the second week of October.

The Chinese believed that after the autumn equinox, yin 陰 began to dominate yang 陽. As the days grew shorter, the dark cold nights gradually lengthened. Since this festival was associated with yin, it was held on the night when the full moon, a female deity worshipped by women, made its appearance in the heavens. The traditional belief was that on the fifteenth day of the eighth moon, the full moon was perfectly round and most beautiful.

This day was also considered a harvest festival since fruits, vegetables and grain had been harvested by this time and food was abundant. With delinquent accounts settled prior to the festival, it was a time for relaxation and celebration. Food offerings were placed on an altar set up in the courtyard. Apples, pears, peaches, grapes, pomegranates, melons, oranges and pomelos might be seen. Special foods for the festival included moon cakes, cooked taro, edible snails 田螺 from the taro patches or rice paddies cooked with sweet basil 紫蘇, and water caltrope 菱角, a type of water chestnut resembling black buffalo horns. Some people insisted that cooked taro be included because at the time of creation, taro was the first food discovered at night in the moonlight. Of all these foods, moon cakes were the most distinctive and could not be omitted from the Mid-Autumn Festival.

The round moon cakes, measuring about three inches in diameter and one and a half inches in thickness, resembled Western fruit cakes in taste and consistency. These cakes were made with melon seeds, lotus seeds, almonds, minced meats, bean paste, orange peels and lard. A golden yolk from a salted duck egg was placed at the center of each cake, and the golden brown crust was decorated with symbols of the festival. Traditionally, thirteen moon cakes were piled in a pyramid to symbolize the thirteen moons of a "complete year"—that is, twelve moons plus one intercalary moon.

The ceremony performed by women to worship the moon was very short. Incense and candles were lighted, and each woman went to the altar to say a short prayer and bow three times. Unlike other ceremonies, firecrackers were not burned at the conclusion. After celebrating the full moon, the family feasted on the fruits, taro, water caltropes, snails, moon cakes, rice soup 粥 and raw fish salad. Children were treated to candy molded into carp, butterflies, and hares.

There were many legends associated with the moon. One popular legend tells the story of the Moon Goddess, Chang O 嫦娥, and her husband, Hou Yi 后羿, who lived during the reign of Emperor Yao 堯, around 2356 B.C. Hou Yi, the Divine Archer, was an officer in the Imperial Guard. One day, nine ravens changed into suns and ten suns appeared in the sky, scorching the earth and making life miserable for people on earth. The emperor commanded Hou Yi to shoot down the nine false suns, a deed which he accomplished with his magic bow and arrow. Hearing of his heroic feat, the Royal Mother of the West 西王母 requested that Hou Yi build her a jade palace. Again Hou Yi performed the task admirably. As a reward, the Royal Mother of the West gave Hou Yi a pill of immortality and instructed him to prepare himself by praying and fasting for one year before taking the pill. Hou Yi hid the pill on a rafter under the roof of his home while undertaking to follow the instructions given him. But before the one year was up, he was summoned to capture a criminal named Chisel Tooth. While he was away on this mission, Chang O noticed a beam of light and the scent of perfume emanating from the rafter. Upon investigation, she discovered the pill and swallowed it. Soon after, she was floating in the air and found that she could fly.

Just then, Hou Yi returned home. Chang O, fearing a severe reprimand, flew out through

Moon Goddess

the window and headed for the moon. Hou Yi followed but was turned back by strong winds. Upon reaching the moon, Chang O immediately coughed up the pill of immortality, which changed into a jade hare. At the same moment, Chang O was transformed into a three-legged toad. To this day, the Chinese imagine that they can see on the moon a three-legged toad and a hare sitting under the sacred cassia tree and preparing the pill of immortality with a mortar and pestle.

Another legend explained the role of the Old Man on the Moon 月老爺, the Divine Matchmaker. The Chinese believed that marriages were made in Heaven but prepared on the moon. The Old Man on the Moon tied the feet of young men and women with red cords for marriage. Thus a maiden made offerings and prayed to him during the Mid-Autumn Festival, hoping that some day she would ride in the red bridal sedan-chair.

Double-Nine Festival

The Double-Nine Festival 重陽節, celebrated on the ninth day of the ninth moon, was the third and final festival for the dead. For this festival, there were many local variations. Some families visited the family graves to worship the ancestors and care for their tombs, although such a visit was not mandatory on this festival. As on the Fourteenth of the Seventh Moon Festival, the ceremony could be performed at the family altar with incense, candles, paper and food offerings, and the burning of color paper representing cloth to be used for clothing. After the ceremony the family gathered for a feast.

Many other activities also took place during the Double-Nine Festival. A custom called "mounting the heights" 登高 coincided with the festival. This custom probably dated from the Han dynasty (206 B.C.–A.D. 220) when sentries were posted on hilltops to prevent thieves from robbing the granaries that were full with the autumn harvest. In one legend, a virtuous scholar named Huan Ching 桓景 was warned by a seer to take food and water and lead his family up a mountain until there was "nothing between him and the sky." The scholar packed food in a bag and chrysanthemum wine in a jug and heeded the advice. When he returned home at the end of the day, he found that all his cattle and poultry were dead. The nature of the calamity was not recorded, but if it had not been for the warning, the scholar and his family un-

doubtedly would have suffered the same fate. People who observed the custom of "mounting the heights" picnicked on a hilltop and drank chrysanthemum wine on the day of Double-Nine. Climbing a hill was taken to be symbolic of success in climbing the ladder of scholarship, advancement and promotions in life. It was also believed that drinking chrysanthemum wine on this day insured longevity.

In southern China, Double-Nine was the day for kite flying. In northern China, by contrast, kites were flown during the third moon. Kites were invented in China during the Sui 隋 dynasty, around A.D. 600, and originally served as signals in times of war. The kites flown on Double-Nine were not toys. They could be very big kites, often requiring four to five strong men to launch and manipulate the kite. Made with bamboo, paper and cloth, the kites varied in size and shape, resembling carp, butterflies, scorpions, centipedes, toads, birds and dragons. When manipulated skillfully, the kites could exhibit lifelike actions such as rolling the eyes, moving the head and paws, flapping or fluttering the wings and wagging the tail. Wind harps were sometimes attached to kites to produce eerie sounds in the sky. Some kites were equipped with hooks and knives to engage in combat with other kites. Sometimes kites were deliberately set adrift in the hope that evil influences hovering about the home would be carried away with the kite and destroyed when it crashed. Kites were even flown at night and the small multicolored lanterns attached to the kite appeared as stars shining in the heavens.

Another amusement on Double-Nine was cricket fighting. Only male crickets were used for fighting, and good fighters were huge, measuring up to four inches in length. Crickets that chirped the loudest were regarded as the best fighters. Each fighting cricket was kept in an earthenware pot equipped with a tiny cup of water for drinking and bathing. These fighters were coddled like fine thoroughbreds. They were fed a diet consisting of two kinds of fish, boiled rice, chestnuts, a certain kind of larva and honey. If they should fall sick, special foods such as mosquitoes, butterflies and shoots from a wild pea were prescribed. Moreover, a charm was placed on the pot to dispel evil influences. The room where the cricket was kept had to be free of smoke, for smoke was injurious to their health and affected their tempers adversely. Even their sex lives were attended to. A fighting cricket was entitled to have a female cricket in his pot for two hours every evening.

On the day of the fight, the crickets were carried in their pots to the arena, which was a circular tub or bowl with a flat bottom. Like prize fighters, crickets were matched according to size and weight. Color could also be a factor. Fighting was induced by tickling their backs with a bristle attached to a small bamboo stick. The fight lasted until one cricket was defeated through either the loss of limbs or the loss of life. Naturally wagers were a considerable part of the fun and excitement.

At the time of Double-Nine, chrysanthemum flowers were brought to a peak of perfection and the autumn crabs were fat and succulent. Scholars held fashionable dinners, ate the delicious crabs, drank chrysanthemum wine, viewed the beautiful blossoms and expressed their joy and contentment by composing poems and couplets.

Winter Solstice Festival

The shortest day of the year, falling on or about December 22 in the Western calendar, was marked by observances in many cultures around the world. Romans, Celts and other Teutonic tribes commemorated this event, and our celebration of Christmas can be traced back to a winter solstice festival. Universally, the winter solstice was regarded as the beginning of the annual reawakening and revival of nature. Henceforth the days would grow longer and the nights shorter.

For the Chinese, the Winter Solstice Festival 冬節 always came during the eleventh month of the lunar calendar and celebrated the beginning of the triumph of yang over yin. On the evening of the solstice, a ceremony was performed at the family altar with incense, candles, offerings and prayers of thanksgiving to Heaven and Earth, the household gods and the spirits of the ancestors. The ancestors were also invited to share in the winter feast. Following the ceremony, the family assembled for a sumptuous dinner.

CHAPTER 6

Popular Gods and Religious Personages

The Chinese pantheon included thousands of gods and religious personages. Although they are too numerous to discuss at any length, some of the more popular ones not treated elsewhere in this book are described here.

Duke of the East

In Chinese mythology, the Duke of the East 東王公 and his wife, the Royal Mother of the West 西王母, represent the first male and female beings. The Duke of the East resides in a misty cloud palace located in the Eastern Heaven, a palace with violet clouds for its dome and blue clouds for its walls. Here the Duke, symbolizing yang 陽, the active or positive male principle, is attended by two servants, Fairy Youth 仙童 and Jade Maiden 玉女. He is the God of the Immortals and keeps a registry listing all the immortals, both male and female.

Royal Mother of the West

The Royal Mother of the West resides in the Western Heaven. Her palace is situated high in the Kun Lun 崑崙 mountains, occupying an area with a circumference of approximately 1,000 *li* 里, or about 333 miles. This palace is also the home of the immortals.

According to the myth, the Royal Mother of the West commanded the Divine Archer and jack-of-all-trades Hou Yi 后羿 to build her a jade palace. The walls surrounding the palace he built are made of gold, and there are twelve jade towers. The palace itself is constructed of multicolored jade. The garden contains incredible fountains that spout jewels instead of water. The peach trees in her magic orchard grow leaves every three thousand years, and another three thousand years elapse before the trees bear fruits that ripen. Eating these peaches confers immortality. When the peaches are ripe, a celestial banquet called the Feast of the Curled Peaches 蟠桃會 is held for all the immortals.

At dinner, the immortals are entertained with sweet, melodious celestial music. The extraordinary menu includes bears' paws, monkeys' lips, dragons' livers and marrow from phoenixes. For dessert, the guests are served the magical peaches to renew their immortality.

Annually on her birthday, which occurs on

Royal Mother of the West

the third day of the third moon, gods and immortals gather at her palace and offer their gifts and congratulations.

The Royal Mother of the West symbolizes yin 陰, the passive or negative female principle. She is often depicted riding a crane and accompanied by two maids, Jade Maiden 玉女 and Spirit Maiden 神女.

Spirits Guarding the Bedroom

There were two spirits that guarded the bedroom. The Duke of the Bed 牀公 was the male spirit, and the Lady of the Bed 牀婆 was the female spirit. Newlyweds and married couples worshipped them. The Duke and Lady of the Bed protected the occupants of the bed and blessed them with many children, especially sons. A temporary altar for worshipping them was usually set on the floor of the bedroom. Incense, tea, wine, cakes and food were offered.

Door Gods

The beautiful colored pictures of the Door Gods 門神 were renewed annually. The old pictures, which were posted on the right and left sides of the front door, were removed and replaced with new ones before the lunar New Year to protect the family from evil spirits, ghosts and demons.

This custom originated with Emperor Tai Tsung 太宗 (627–650) of the T'ang 唐 dynasty. According to legend, the emperor was suffering from a strange malady. During the day he was apparently well but at night he was bothered by ghosts and demons. He saw and heard them in his bedroom. They also threw bricks against the walls and made weird noises outside his bedroom. These disturbances caused him to be feverish, and his physical and mental health deteriorated. The court physicians were baffled and did not know how to treat the unusual disorder. His family and his ministers were concerned that his life was in jeopardy.

Two brave generals, Chin Shu-Pao 秦叔寶 and Hu Ching-Te 胡敬德, who were not afraid of evil spirits, ghosts and demons, volunteered to stand watch outside the front gate of the palace. They protected the emperor and prevented the evil spirits from disturbing his sleep at night. The apparitions and weird noises ceased. The emperor's health gradually improved as long as the two generals continued their vigilance. Feeling sorry for his loyal generals who also needed their sleep at night, the emperor ordered the court painter to paint their pictures in full armor complete with battle axes, chains, whips, bows and arrows. The portraits of the two fierce-looking generals replaced the men and were posted on the right and left sides of the palace front gate. For a while, with the portraits beside the front gate, all was well. The emperor's health was fully restored.

Later the disturbances recurred because the evil spirits gained entrance to the palace through the back gate, causing the emperor to have a relapse. Minister Wei Cheng 魏徵 volunteered to stand watch at night at the back gate, and his vigil thwarted the ghosts and demons at the back gate.

The colorful paintings of the Door Gods depicted Chin Shu-Pao with a white face and Hu Ching-Te with a black face. Wei Cheng was also considered a Door God and was often pictured with Chin and Hu. At times he replaced them.

God of Wealth

The God of Wealth 財神 was universally worshipped throughout China. His picture was found in most homes and shops, for he was the special patron of merchants. At the end of the year, the year-old portrait of the God of Wealth was removed and burned. On the third day of the new year, a new picture was posted and ceremonies were performed to welcome and honor him. In addition, poor people and gamblers worshipped him on the twentieth day of the seventh moon.

There was a considerable difference of opinion regarding his origin and identity. The most popular legend claimed that the God of Wealth

was a deified hermit named Chao Kung-Ming 趙公明, who lived around the beginning of the Chou 周 dynasty. As the story goes, one Chiang Tzu-Ya 姜子牙 was fighting for Wu Wang 武王 of the Chou dynasty against the last emperor of the Shang 商 dynasty around 1121 to 1114 B.C. One of Chiang's adversaries was Chao Kung-Ming, a person of infinite resources and sagacity who was able to perform feats of magic. He could ride a black tiger and hurl pearls that burst like bombshells. To neutralize his magic, Chiang Tzu-Ya made a straw doll of Chao Kung-Ming and worshipped it for twenty days. On the twenty-first day, he shot out the doll's eyes and heart with arrows made of peach wood, causing Chao to faint, become ill and then be killed in battle.

God of Wealth

Later Chiang Tzu-Ya petitioned the Supreme God of Taoism 元始天尊 to free from hell 地獄 all the spirits of heroes who had died in battle. When Chao Kung-Ming was presented, he was praised for his bravery and honored as the head of the Ministry of Riches and Prosperity, the God of Wealth.

The God of Wealth was often pictured as a man under a money tree with leaves of coins, surrounded by gold, silver and other treasures, and accompanied by attendants also laden with treasures.

Kitchen God

The Kitchen God 竈君 was also known as the Spirit of the Hearth 竈神, the King of the Hearth 竈王 and the Duke of the Hearth 竈公. This god resided in the kitchen near the stove and was worshipped by both Taoists and Buddhists. He was worshipped at the end of the year when he left for Heaven to report on the family's conduct during the year and again just before the beginning of the new year, when he returned to his post.

There was no agreement regarding his origin and identity. A popular legend claimed that he was Chang Tsao-Wang 張竈王, who had been married to a pure, chaste and virtuous woman, Kuo Ting-Hsiang 郭丁香. This union resulted in good fortune and prosperity for the family, but later, when Chang left his good wife and married a licentious woman, Li Hai-Tang 李海棠, Kuo Ting-Hsiang returned to the home of her parents. Chang's second marriage resulted in bad luck and misfortune. He was poverty stricken, lost his eyesight and became a beggar.

One day, while begging for food and alms, he

Kitchen God

unknowingly came to the home of Kuo Ting-Hsiang. She recognized her former husband, invited him in and prepared a bowl of his favorite noodles. Eating the noodles, he recalled the past and started to cry. He told her that his good wife, whom he had left, used to prepare his noodles exactly the same way. She told him to open his eyes. He opened them and, to his great surprise, found that his vision was restored. Seeing Ting-Hsiang, he was overcome with shame and tried to hide behind the nearby hearth. In doing so, he inadvertently fell into the fire. Ting-Hsiang tried to save him. She grasped one of his legs and pulled—the leg separated from the body. The rest of the body remained in the fire, and Chang Tsao-Wang was burned to death. To mourn the death of Chang Tsao-Wang and honor his spirit, Ting-Hsiang placed his tablet behind the hearth and worshipped it.

The Kitchen God watched over the family. He was responsible for determining a long or short life span and the wealth or poverty of its members; he also recorded their deeds, good or bad, during the year. Cooks celebrated his birthday on the third day of the eighth moon.

God of Joy

The God of Joy 喜神 was not thought to have been a particular individual and was depicted in many ways. He was sometimes shown carrying a basket or a sieve planted with three arrows. He was also seen carried on the shoulders of the God of Wealth and holding the character for joy, *hsi* 喜. He was again depicted with a big smile, dressed in green, holding the same character or piling gold and silver bullion in a large basket. A picture of the God of Joy was used as a talisman to dispel evil spirits. For example, a picture of him was placed in front of the red bridal sedan-chair to protect the bride while en route from her home to the home of her future husband.

God of Happiness

The God of Happiness 福神 was usually shown as an old gentleman with a high forehead, dressed in a blue robe, leading his little son to court. This god was revered and worshipped almost as much as the God of Wealth.

Emperor Wu Ti 武帝 (502–550) of the Liang 梁 dynasty forced the dwarfs and comedians from the district of Tao Chou 道州 to serve him. He made the dwarfs his slaves and the comedians his entertainers. This caused considerable hardship and unhappiness among the people of the district. Judge Yang Cheng 陽城 was informed of the situation. He told the emperor that according to law, the dwarfs and comedians were his subjects and not his slaves and entertainers. He advised the emperor to free them. Following the judge's opinion, the dwarfs and comedians were freed and their forced bondage terminated.

The people of Tao Chou were overjoyed and offered sacrifices to Judge Yang Cheng. Eventually he was deified as the God of Happiness.

God of Official Pay

The God of Official Pay 祿神 was considered a secondary God of Wealth. This god was the deified scholar Shih Fen 石奮, a high official in the court of Emperor Ching Ti 景帝 of the Han 漢 dynasty, who reigned from 156 to 140 B.C. While in office, Shih Fen had been paid large sums of money, and he and other members of his family became extremely wealthy.

Star God of Longevity

The Star God of Longevity was originally the Star of Longevity 壽星. The first emperor of China, Chin Shih Huang Ti 秦始皇帝 (221–206 B.C.), offered sacrifices to it. Later it was claimed that the Star of Longevity had descended to earth and assumed a human form. Thus he became the Star God of Longevity 壽星公.

The three Star Gods: God of Happiness, God of Official Pay and God of Longevity

The Star God of Longevity was easy to identify. Depicted as a smiling, happy old man with a large and bulging forehead, he was shown riding on a stag or leaning on a staff. With him were other symbols of longevity, including bats, peaches, gourds with medicines, scrolls, deer, Manchurian cranes and pine trees.

The God of Happiness, the God of Official Pay and the Star God of Longevity were often referred to collectively as the Three Stars 福祿壽三星.

City God

The City God, or Cheng Huang 城隍, was an Earth God whose jurisdiction covered an entire town or city. He was regarded as the spiritual protector of the area. The term Cheng Huang was derived from the fortifications of the city. Every fortified city was encircled by a high wall, or *cheng* 城. The wall, an embankment of earth, was often faced with stone. A moat, or *huang* 隍, usually filled with water, surrounded the wall. It was believed that the spirit of the City God resided in the wall and moat. The birthday of the City God was celebrated on the twenty-fifth day of the ninth moon. Incense, prayers and other offerings were presented, and processions were held to honor him.

There was a difference of opinion as to when the City God was first worshipped. Some claimed that the worship dated back to Emperor Yao 堯 (2356–2255 B.C.). Others maintained that it began with the ruler Ta Ti 大帝 of the kingdom of Wu 吳, who around A.D. 222 worshipped the Spirit of the Land. Nevertheless, since the Sung 宋 dynasty (960–1279), sacrifices to the City God were offered throughout China. The City God had many duties. He was responsible for the peace and welfare of the city. He controlled demons and protected the city against storms, floods, droughts, plagues, epidemics and other calamities. As with the local Earth God, anyone who performed outstanding and meritorious service might be chosen for deification as a City God.

There were many City Gods. One of the most famous was the warrior and hero Yo Fei 岳飛, who lived from 1103 to 1141. Yo Fei was born in Hunan 湖南 province during the Sung dynasty. It was reported that his birth was announced by a huge bird, probably a swan, that flew over his home and alighted on the roof. Because of this, he was named Fei, meaning "to fly." His parents were kind and generous. Although they were poor, they shared their food and lent their land to the needy. Yo Fei developed into a noted archer and became a general who commanded a cavalry unit under the Sung emperor. When the Chin 金, known as the "Golden Tartars," descended from the north and invaded the Sung empire, even Yo Fei, with his brilliant cavalry tactics, was unable to prevent them from occupying the northern provinces. The Sung emperor and his father were captured at Kaifeng 開封.

The younger brother of the captured emperor assumed the Sung throne. He fled south with his court and established a new capital at the city of Hangchow 杭州. The new emperor selected Chin Kuei 秦檜 to be his prime minister, but it proved to be a bad choice. Chin Kuei was bribed by the Chin invaders and turned against the throne. To help the Chin, Chin Kuei vilified Yo Fei and prevented him from carrying out his plan to recapture the lost territories and rescue the Sung emperor and his father from the enemy.

Yo Fei was arrested, imprisoned and charged with treason. During the trial, he ripped off his jacket and revealed to the court four characters on his back: 盡忠報國, meaning "Complete devotion to the country." These characters had been tattooed by his mother. Yo Fei was acquitted, but later he was rearrested and murdered in a prison at Hangchow. After the death of Yo Fei, the truth came out. Chin Kuei and his wife were unmasked, denounced and disgraced. The next emperor decreed that Yo Fei was henceforth to be considered a national hero. All his titles were restored, and he was awarded the posthumous title "Loyal and

Yo Fei

Heroic" 忠烈. He was eventually deified as the City God of Hangchow.

In the twelfth century, the people of Hangchow constructed a tomb and a temple 岳王廟 to honor him. Located not far from the shore of Hangchow's beautiful West Lake 西湖, the tomb and temple have been restored recently. The main temple houses the statue of Yo Fei. The ceiling of the hall is decorated with cranes, a symbol of longevity. There are two pavilions, one on each side of the courtyard, each containing a statue of an officer. The two officers are Yo Fei's comrades in arms who were executed with him. West of the courtyard are two rounded tombs. The large tomb contains only the clothing of Yo

Fei, because his body was lost. The smaller tomb is the grave of his son, Yo Yun 岳雲.

The path leading to the tombs is lined with stone statues of lions, rams, horses and civil servants. Facing the tomb of Yo Fei are four cast iron statues representing Chin Kuei, his wife, a jealous general and the head of the prison where Yo Fei was incarcerated. Since they were responsible for the arrest, imprisonment and murder of Yo Fei, the four conspirators are shown kneeling with their hands tied behind their backs, as if awaiting execution. In the past, visitors to the tomb of Yo Fei expressed their contempt for the four traitors by kicking the statues, beating them with sticks or spitting on them.

Five Thunder Spirits

The Celestial Ministry of Thunder and Storms 雷部 was assigned by the Dragon King 龍王 to control the weather. This ministry was staffed with more than eighty officials, chief among them being the Five Thunder Spirits 五雷神, namely, the Ancestor of Thunder 雷祖, the Duke of Thunder 雷公, the Mother of Lightning 電母, the God of Wind 風伯 and the Master of Rain 雨師. These Thunder Spirits were popular gods often found in temples.

Ancestor of Thunder

The Ancestor of Thunder was the head of the Celestial Ministry. He was depicted as a god with three eyes. The third eye was in the middle of his forehead, and when opened, it emitted a beam of light. His birthday was celebrated on the twenty-sixth day of the sixth moon.

According to legend, the Ancestor of Thunder was originally Minister Wen Chung 聞仲, who lived at the end of the Shang 商 dynasty, around 1100 B.C. Although a courageous warrior in battle against the Chou 周, he was forced to retreat to the mountains, where he encountered a powerful adversary, Marshal Yun Chung-Tzu 雲中子.

The marshal used his magic to produce lightning and mysterious columns of fire which surrounded Wen Chung. Each column of fire

Ancestor of Thunder

was thirty feet in height and ten feet in diameter. From each column, ninety fiery dragons emerged and flew into the air. The sky was like a furnace. Trapped in the fire, Wen Chung was burned to death.

The next dynasty, the Chou, honored him for his valor and gallantry. He was elevated to a Celestial Prince and assigned the duty of distributing clouds and rain.

Duke of Thunder

Prior to the introduction of Buddhism into China in the first century A.D., the Duke of Thunder was depicted as a man holding a chisel and a hammer. Later, he became a creature with wings and birdlike features. People who saw him described him as having batlike wings. His head resembled a monkey with a dark blue face, his mouth was large and beaklike and his feet were clawed. He held a hammer in one hand and a chisel in the other. With the hammer, he beat the celestial drums strung around his body to produce loud thunder claps. The chisel was used to kill people by driving it through their heads.

It is probably the case that after the introduction of Buddhism, the Chinese changed the image of the Duke of Thunder to resemble Vajrapani, the Indian Rain God who had the wings of a Garuda, a mythical golden-winged vulture that was half-bird and half-man.

The Chinese believed that the Duke of Thunder punished and killed people who wasted food. Those who threw rice on the ground and trampled it were likely to know his wrath. Yet, although he occasionally killed people, the Duke of Thunder was considered a benevolent god who provided protection from evil spirits.

He also helped to dispense the rain which was so essential for a bountiful harvest.

Mother of Lightning

The Mother of Lightning was a goddess dressed in blue, green, red and white robes. She held a mirror in each hand and, by manipulating the mirrors, produced lightning. She assisted the Duke of Thunder by directing the lightning to the culprits; then he could, with accuracy, punish them by driving his chisel through their heads. The Chinese belief was that people were killed by thunder, not by lightning.

God of Wind

The God of Wind was depicted as an old man with a long white beard, dressed in a yellow cloak and wearing a red and blue hat. He held a large bag of wind and, by pointing the mouth of the bag, controlled the direction and the velocity of the wind.

Master of Rain

The Master of Rain was depicted as a man dressed in yellow armor and wearing a blue and yellow hat. He stood on the clouds dispensing rain either by pouring water from a watering can or by sprinkling water from an earthen bowl with leaves from a tree branch.

Monkey God

The Monkey God 孫猴子 was also known as the Seeker of Space 孫悟空, the Great Sage

Equal to Heaven 齊天大聖 and the Mischievous Monkey 馬騮精. He was worshipped by Taoists and Buddhists on the twenty-third day of the second moon. It was believed that the Monkey God was able to bestow good health and insure success—through his supernatural powers he could overcome the goblins, witches and malevolent spirits that caused illness and failure.

The Monkey God had little to do with the yellow monkeys found near the borderlands of Tibet or the golden monkeys living in the provinces of Szechuan 四川 and Kansu 甘肅. He was rather the invention of a sixteenth-century writer with a fertile imagination. His book, *Record of a Journey to the West* 西遊記, was based on the famous pilgrimage of the Buddhist monk Tang Seng 唐僧, whose religious name was Hsuan Chuang 玄奘, during the reign of Emperor Tai Tsung 太宗 of the Tang 唐 dynasty. Tang Seng left the capital city of Changan 長安, later renamed Sian 西安, in 629 and traveled westward to India with the intention of bringing back to China copies of the Buddhist sutras. The *Record of a Journey to the West* is a delightful novel filled with humor, nonsense, fantasy and good-natured satire.

As the story has it, a rock on a mountain was formed in the shape of an egg at the time of creation. The rock absorbed the essence of Heaven, the savors of Earth, the vigor of sunshine, the grace of the moonbeams and the breath of the winds until at length a monkey emerged from the rock-egg complete in every organ and limb. This monkey became king of the monkeys and eventually learned enough magic to become an immortal. He was able to change his shape into 72 different forms, leap 180,000 *li* 里, or about 60,000 miles, and ride on

Monkey God

the clouds. He could chew a handful of his hair, spit out the fragments and transform them into several hundred monkeys. From the Dragon King of the Eastern Sea 東海龍王 he obtained an iron rod which on command could expand to 20 feet in length and be used as a weapon, or could shrink to the size of an embroidery needle and be comfortably kept behind his ear.

This mischievous monkey with supernatural powers caused all kinds of disturbances on earth and in Heaven. The Jade Emperor 玉皇 summoned him to Heaven to explain his irresponsible conduct, but while in Heaven he continued to be unruly, stealing the peaches of immortality and eating them. He then proclaimed himself to be the Great Sage Equal to Heaven.

To punish him for his bad behavior, the Buddha imprisoned him on a remote mountaintop in a magic jail.

There the monkey eventually repented. Hearing this, the Goddess of Mercy 觀音菩薩 released him from the prison after he further vowed to devote himself to Buddhism and to accompany the monk Tang Seng on his pilgrimage. To control the unpredictable monkey, the Goddess of Mercy placed a band around his head which, on Tang Seng's command, would constrict and cause the monkey excruciating pain.

On their journey to the West, Tang Seng and the monkey encountered two other pilgrims, Pig Fairy 猪八戒 and Sandy the Monk 沙和尚, with whom they joined forces on the long trek to India. Pig Fairy was an immortal who had been driven out of Heaven for abusing the daughter of the Jade Emperor. On earth, his soul entered the body of a pig and he promptly became half-pig and half-human. His head and ears were those of a pig while his body was that of a man. Like Pig Fairy, Sandy the Monk had been exiled from Heaven by the Jade Emperor, for breaking a crystal bowl holding the peaches of immortality at a celestial banquet. On earth, he lived along the banks of the Flowing Sand River 流沙河. Both Pig Fairy and Sandy the Monk were converted to Buddhism by the Goddess of Mercy, and they too vowed to protect Tang Seng on his perilous journey.

The pilgrims encountered many dangers along the way, including gales, floods, fires, carnal temptations and cold and hunger. They fought many battles. The monkey used the iron rod kept behind his ear to fight off numerous adversaries. With his magical powers and with help from Pig Fairy and Sandy the Monk, the monkey at last made good his vow to conduct Tang Seng safely to the holy Buddhist shrines in India.

When the pilgrims finally returned to Sian with the Buddhist sutras, the emperor and his subjects greeted them with great enthusiasm. They were showered with gifts and the overjoyed emperor ordered a lavish dinner prepared to honor them. In Heaven, all the gods were called to a meeting with the Buddha. They decided that the four pilgrims and the white horse that had carried Tang Seng and the sutras should be elevated to the heavenly ranks. Tang Seng and the monkey became Buddhas. Pig Fairy was appointed Chief Altar-Washer of the gods, and Sandy the Monk was promoted to the rank of a Worthy. The white horse was transformed into a celestial dragon.

The Monkey God then requested that his head-constricting band be removed. Tang Seng asked if he was sure that the band was still around his head. He raised his hand to check—and to his great surprise, the band had mysteriously disappeared.

Episodes from the *Record of a Journey to the West* have entertained the Chinese for over three hundred years and have served as themes for storytellers, operas and motion pictures.

Dragons

In the West dragons have usually been regarded as horrible monsters. Believed to inhabit unknown parts of the world, they were depicted as fire-breathing serpents with wings, able to swallow men and ships in one gulp. In Christian theology, dragons represent sin, evil and destruction. It was this kind of dragon that St. George, the patron saint of England, slew with Ascalon, his magic sword.

In contrast, the Chinese have generally considered the dragon 龍 to be benevolent. The dragon symbolized yang, the active or positive male principle, and it stood for fertility, vigilance, strength and imperial power. Since ancient times, the dragon was regarded as the first of the four supernatural animals, the others being the unicorn 麟, the phoenix 鳳 and the tortoise 龜.

The Chinese believed that there were innumerable dragons, varying in color, size and power. An azure or blue dragon symbolized the east and was identified with spring. Red or yellow dragons represented the south and summer. A white dragon was associated with the west and autumn, while a black dragon stood for the north and winter.

Many dragon myths have been recorded. Dragons were able, at will, to shrink to the size of a silkworm or expand to fill the space between Heaven and Earth. Living in the rivers, lakes and oceans, they ascended to Heaven in the spring and reappeared as clouds and rain. They returned at the autumn equinox, descending into the water and burying themselves in the mud. Buddhists held that the number of dragons was equal to the number of fishes in the sea, for fish and serpents were capable of changing into dragons through patient exertion and suffering. They also believed that not all dragons lived in the water, and that those inhabiting the hills or hovering around graves were not entirely benevolent.

The most popular dragon was the Dragon King 龍王, considered the Dispenser of Rain. During the fifth and sixth moons, and especially on his birthday, the thirteenth day of the sixth moon, dragon processions were held throughout China to insure a favorable response to prayers for rain. If there was no rain during the summer months, the image of the Dragon King would be exposed to the blazing sun to induce him to bring forth rain. In times of drought, everyone from peasants to ministers and even the emperor himself offered special sacrifices and prayed to the Dragon King for relief.

The dragon stood for power, especially imperial power. The symbol of a five-clawed dragon was reserved for the emperor and princes of the first and second ranks. Five-clawed dragons therefore decorated the emperor's palaces, thrones, robes, household articles, flags and umbrellas. Princes of lower ranks and ministers were entitled to a dragon with four claws, and commoners were limited to dragons with three claws. During the Ming 明 dynasty (1368–1644), the national color was red and the imperial crest was a red dragon. The Ching 清 dynasty (1644–1911) changed the national color to yellow and the imperial crest became a yellow or golden dragon.

Dragon

The Chinese usually depicted the dragon as a composite animal. It had the head of a camel, the horns of a deer, the eyes of a rabbit, the body and neck of a snake, the belly of a frog, four legs with the claws of a hawk, the palms of a tiger and the scales of a carp. Eighty-one ridges could be counted along its back, and there were whiskers on each side of the mouth, a beard under its chin and a round object in front of the chin. This round object was variously explained: it was the sun, the moon, an egg, a pearl or the emblem of yin and yang. The dragon's breath came out as clouds and could change into water or even fire. The sound of its voice was said to resemble the jingling of copper coins, although the dragon itself was deaf. Interestingly, the Chinese character for "deaf" 聾 shows a dragon over the ear and has the same pronunciation as the word for dragon, *lung*.

Provider of Children

The Provider of Children, Chang Hsien 張仙, was an immortal who protected families from the Celestial Dog 天狗. It was believed that if a family came under the Celestial Dog's influence, they would have no sons or the sons would be short-lived.

In one legend, Emperor Jen Tsung 仁宗 (1023–1064) of the Sung dynasty dreamt of a man with unusually white skin and black hair who carried a bow and arrow in his hand. This man, Chang Hsien, informed the emperor that the Celestial Dog was hiding behind the sun and moon as the Dog-Star 狗星. This Celestial Dog came down to earth and devoured little children but his presence had kept the wicked animal away. After awakening, the emperor de-

Provider of Children

creed that a portrait of Chang Hsien should be painted and worshipped.

In another legend, the Provider of Children was originally named Chang Yuan-Hsiao 張遠霄 and was a native of Szechuan province. One day, he met a very old man with two eyeballs in each eye. The old man carried a bamboo crossbow and three iron arrows which he offered to sell for three hundred strings of cash. Chang Yuan-Hsiao bought the bow and arrows without any hesitation. Then the old man informed him that the bow and arrows had the power to dispel evil spirits and epidemics. Later the old man helped Chang become an immortal.

The Provider of Children has been worshipped since the Sung dynasty. Women who desired children hung his portrait in their bedroom, for he was also regarded as the patron of childbearing women. He was usually depicted as a man with a white face and long beard, holding a bow and arrow to fend off the Celestial Dog. He was usually accompanied by a little boy at his side.

Vanquisher of Hell

The Chinese did not believe in an everlasting hell. They believed that sinners, regardless of their misdeeds, were eventually released from hell. However, some might be released sooner than others.

The Vanquisher of Hell was named Ti-Tsang Wang 地藏王. He was a merciful god who descended into hell, rescued the souls suffering there and led them to Heaven. He was sometimes depicted as a god with eighteen arms, suggesting his ability to save innumerable souls. He was also depicted as a god with a round face who held in one hand a staff topped with six rings, used to open the gates of hell, and in his other hand a jewel which emitted the light of salvation. He was worshipped on the thirtieth day of the seventh moon, the day the hungry ghosts returned to hell.

According to legend, in the reign of Emperor Su Tsung 肅宗 (756–763) of the Tang dynasty, Ti-Tsang Wang was a person named Chin Chiao-Chio 金喬覺 who came from the little kingdom of Hsin Lo 新羅, in present-day Korea. Although born a prince and brought up in luxury, he had renounced worldly life and had become a wandering monk called Mu Lien 目連. One day his wanderings brought him to a mountain near the south bank of the Yangtze River 揚子江 in Anhui 安徽 province. This mountain had been named the Nine Flowered Mountain 九華山 by the celebrated poet Li Tai-Po 李太白, who had viewed it from the river and thought that the mountain peaks resembled the nine upturned petals of a lotus flower. Mu Lien lived in a very small hut on this mountain. Here he meditated and taught the disciples who gathered around him. It was said that Li Tai-Po himself came to see Mu Lien.

One day while meditating, Mu Lien had a vision in which it was revealed that his mother, in hell, was hungry. Mu Lien gathered some food and descended into hell. However, hungry ghosts managed to steal the food before he could find her. He tried again but still did not find her. After a long search, he finally discovered that his mother had been reincarnated as a dog. Eventually he found the dog and took care of it with great affection.

Mu Lien lived to be ninety-nine. He died sitting with his legs crossed and surrounded by his disciples. Three years later, when his coffin was opened, his body was just as fresh as when he had died. In time he was deified as the Vanquisher of Hell.

Jade Emperor

The Jade or Pearly Emperor, Yu Huang 玉皇, was the Supreme Ruler of Heaven 上帝.

Although he was a popular and familiar personage in Chinese mythology, his origins remain unclear. Some have claimed that he was originally the Hindu god Indra, whom the Taoists adopted and renamed the Jade Emperor. Others maintained that he had once been a mortal prince.

According to this legend, King Ching Te 淨德 and Queen Pao Yueh 寶月 of the ancient kingdom of Kuang-Yen Miao-Lo Kuo 光嚴妙樂國 were unable to produce a male heir to succeed to the throne. They consulted Taoist priests, offered incense and prayed to the gods for help to correct the problem. Subsequently the queen conceived after having a vision of the sage Lao Tzu 老子, the founder of Taoism. In this vision Lao Tzu was carrying a male child while riding on the back of a tiger. Descending through the clouds, Lao Tzu presented the child to her. The queen gave birth to a prince. As a child the young prince was unusually kind and generous to the poor and the needy. When the king died, the prince assumed the throne, but after ruling for only a few days, he decided to relinquish it. He devoted the remainder of his life to healing the sick, saving lives and performing virtuous deeds.

According to another account, the Jade Emperor was invented by Emperor Chen Tsung 眞宗 (998–1023) of the Sung dynasty. This emperor signed an unpopular peace treaty with the barbarians from the north, Tungus and Kitans, who had invaded the Sung empire. To regain the support of his subjects, he assembled his ministers and proclaimed that he was in direct contact with the Supreme Ruler of Heaven, the Jade Emperor. He ordered that an image be made of the Jade Emperor and commanded his court to worship this newly created god.

In 1115, Emperor Hui Tsung 徽宗, also of the Sung dynasty, built a temple dedicated to the Jade Emperor. He also decreed that similar temples be built throughout the land, so that all the people of China could honor and worship the Supreme Ruler of Heaven.

The Jade Emperor was a very personal god. As Supreme Ruler of Heaven, he supervised the affairs of the world and gods of lower rank reported to him regularly. His birthday was celebrated on the ninth day of the first moon.

Mi-Lo Fo

A popular Buddha often displayed in temples was Mi-Lo Fo 彌勒佛. He was known as the Happy Buddha 喜佛 or the Laughing Buddha 笑佛 because of his big broad smile. He was also known as the Buddha with the Calico Bag 布袋佛.

It was said that Mi-Lo Fo had been an Indian prince who after death met Sakyamuni Buddha 釋迦牟尼佛, the founder of Buddhism, in Heaven. The Buddha appointed Mi-Lo Fo to be the "Coming Buddha." He knew that three thousand years after his death, the world would be totally corrupt and the Buddhist Law would no longer be remembered or obeyed. Mi-Lo Fo would then return as the "Coming Buddha" to explain the Buddhist teachings once again and to remind people to observe them.

Mi-Lo Fo was worshipped because of his merciful and compassionate nature. His anniversary was celebrated on the third day of the sixth moon. Since the Yuan 元 dynasty (1279–1368), Mi-Lo Fo has been depicted as a fat man with a big broad smile and long ear lobes reaching to his shoulders. Sitting on the ground with his robe casually draped over his body, exposing his breast and upper abdomen,

Mi-Lo Fo

he holds a calico bag in his left hand. His left leg is bent at the knee. Some believed that the calico bag was a magical bag holding "primitive ether" 氣母, the germ of the past world. Others claimed that the bag held his food and all his earthly belongings. In his right hand, he holds his prayer beads or a lotus bud. He was often depicted with little children clinging to him.

O-Mi-To Fo

O-Mi-To Fo 阿彌陀佛 is the Chinese pronunciation of the Sanskrit name Amitabha, meaning "Buddha of Boundless Light." In China he was a very popular Buddha from the fifth century on. His anniversary was celebrated on the seventh day of the eleventh moon.

His origins are obscure. Some thought he was the incarnation of the ninth son of an ancient Buddha. Others believed that he had been a powerful ruler who gave up his throne to become a monk. This monk made forty-eight vows. One was that he would become a Buddha only on the condition that he could establish a paradise where every living being who believed in him and called his name could enjoy a happy existence. In this paradise, favorable conditions would make it possible for souls to attain nirvana directly, without having to go through the many rebirths which would ordinarily be required. Many Buddhists believed that only two things were necessary to attain entry into O-Mi-To Fo's paradise: faith in his vow, and the repeated chanting of his name.

It was said that O-Mi-To Fo resided in the Western Paradise 西天. He was usually depicted as a Buddha with short curly hair, long-lobed ears and extremely long hands. He was either standing or sitting on a lotus throne accompanied by one of his disciples.

Eight Immortals

Immortals or *hsien* 仙 were supernatural beings invented by the fertile imagination of the Taoists. They were not gods but fairies. Taoists believed that human beings could, through arduous study, learn the secrets of nature and conquer death. As immortals these beings lived in the remote hills and on mountaintops. Their souls were able to leave and return to their bodies, and they could be visible or invisible at will. They were also able to transmute metal into gold, revive the dead, fly through the air, ride on the clouds, walk on the ocean waves, set the ocean afire, assume different forms and enjoy eternal bliss.

The most famous immortals were the Eight Immortals 八仙, sometimes known as the Eight Inebriated Immortals 酒中八仙, who probably entered the popular culture during the Yuan 元 dynasty. The Eight Immortals, singly or collectively, signified happiness. They stood for different conditions of life such as wealth and poverty, youth and old age, masculinity and femininity, the aristocrat and the commoner. Of the eight, six were males, one was female and one was of indeterminate sex. Three were thought to be historical personages and the remaining five were products of pure fantasy.

There were many tales extolling the feats of the Eight Immortals, either singly or as a group. One popular story told of the "Eight Immortals Crossing the Sea" 八仙過海 to explore the wonderful things in the sea which could not be found in Heaven. There they encountered the Dragon King of the Eastern Sea 東海龍王, who tried to steal their magical instruments and imprison them. The story recounts their victorious battles against the Dragon King and other sea adventures.

The Eight Immortals are described below in the chronological order of their inception.

Li Tieh-Kuai

Li Tieh-Kuai 李鐵拐 was the first and the most popular of the Eight Immortals. According to legend, his parents died when he was very young and he was mistreated by his sister-in-law. As a result, his childhood was difficult and unhappy. The Royal Mother of the West took him under her care, treated a chronic festering ulcer on his leg and taught him how to become an immortal.

One day his soul left his body to visit Hua Shan 華山, one of the sacred mountains of China. He instructed his disciple to cremate his body if he did not return after seven days. However, because the disciple's mother was dying and he was in a hurry to leave for home, he cremated Li Tieh-Kuai's body on the sixth day. When the soul of Li Tieh-Kuai returned on the seventh day, he did not find his body. All he found was a heap of ashes. The only body he could find for his soul to enter was the corpse of a beggar who had just died of hunger. The dead beggar had a pointed head, black face, huge eyes, unruly hair, long beard and a crippled leg.

Animating the beggar's body and carrying an iron crutch which the sage Lao Tzu, the founder of Taoism, had given him, Li Tieh-Kuai

Eight Immortals crossing the sea

proceeded to see his disciple's dead mother. He poured a magical medication from his gourd into her mouth and the woman came back to life. Then with a gust of wind, Li Tieh-Kuai mysteriously disappeared.

Li Tieh-Kuai was the patron of pharmacists and was usually depicted as a cripple supported by an iron crutch. At times he was shown standing on a crab or accompanied by a deer.

Chung Li-Chuan

Chung Li-Chuan 鍾離權 was able to change copper and pewter into silver with the use of mysterious drugs. The silver was then given to the poor.

One day while he was meditating, the stone wall of his mountain home disintegrated, exposing a jade casket. In it he found the secret of how to become an immortal. He followed the instructions and soon his room was filled with multicolored clouds and sweet music. In another instant he was transformed into an immortal, and was carried away on the back of a celestial stork.

Chung Li-Chuan was usually depicted as a stout man holding a peach in one hand and a feather fan in the other hand. This magical fan was used to revive the dead.

Lan Tsai-Ho

Lan Tsai-Ho 藍采和 was a stout but mentally deranged street singer who had no regard for money. Since the gender of this immortal was undetermined, Lan Tsai-Ho was probably a hermaphrodite.

The patron of florists, Lan Tsai-Ho was usually shown dressed in a blue gown with one foot bare and one foot shod, carrying a basket of flowers.

Chang Kuo-Lao

Chang Kuo-Lao 張果老 was a recluse born in Shansi 山西 province sometime in the seventh or eighth century. He had a supernatural white mule on which he was able to travel great distances. He preferred to mount the mule backwards so that he rode facing the tail of the animal. When the mule was not in use, he folded the animal and tucked it away like a sheet of paper. When he wanted to travel, he squirted the sheet with a little water and the mule reappeared.

Since it was said that he was old at birth, he symbolized old age. He was usually depicted carrying a fish drum 魚鼓, a hollow bamboo drum struck with two sticks. Pictures of Chang Kuo-Lao offering a son were frequently hung in bridal chambers.

Ho Hsien-Ku

Ho Hsien-Ku 何仙姑 was the daughter of a storekeeper who lived in the seventh century in Hunan province. Living alone on a remote hill, she survived on powdered mother-of-pearl and moonbeams. She was said to have attained immortality after eating a magical peach.

Lu Tung-Pin

Lu Tung-Pin 呂洞賓 was born in Shansi province around the middle of the eighth century. He was a high official who fell into disfavor and sought refuge in the mountains. There he studied alchemy. With his supernatural powers, he helped to eliminate the world of evil and offensive dragons. At the age of fifty, he became an immortal.

Lu Tung-Pin was the patron of barbers and

scholars. He was depicted carrying a devil-slaying saber and a fly-whisk which he used to master space.

Han Hsiang-Tzu

Han Hsiang-Tzu 韓湘子 was a disciple of Lu Tung-Pin who attained immortality after falling off a magical peach tree. He was able to bring forth plants from areas with no soil and made them bloom immediately. He was the patron of musicians and was depicted carrying a basket of flowers and a jade flute.

Tsao Kuo-Chiu

Tsao Kuo-Chiu 曹國舅 was a military commander and brother of an empress. His brother-in-law was Emperor Jen Tsung 仁宗 (1023–1064) of the Sung dynasty.

Ashamed because his younger brother was guilty of murder, he hid in the mountains and clothed his body with leaves from wild plants. Living as a hermit, he learned the secrets of nature and attained immortality.

Tsao Kuo-Chiu was the patron of actors. He was usually depicted dressed in official court robes and holding a pair of castanets made from court tablets.

CHAPTER 7

Chinese Philosophers

Great thinkers throughout history have meditated on the nature of man, his fate, his relationship to his fellow man and his role within the vast universe. There have been many outstanding Chinese philosophers who have expounded their ideas on these subjects. The three best known are Lao Tzu, Confucius and Mencius, who all lived during the golden age of Chinese philosophy in the Chou 周 dynasty. Their concepts have influenced the thinking and behavior of the Chinese up to the present day.

Lao Tzu

Very little is known about Lao Tzu 老子, the traditional founder of Taoism. Accounts of his birth, life and death are legendary rather than historical. Lao Tzu was supposedly carried in his mother's womb for eighty years before birth. At birth he looked like an old man with snowy white hair and a long beard. He was therefore called Lao Tzu, meaning "Old Master." It was said that he was born in 604 B.C., making him an older contemporary of Confucius. His surname was Li 李 and his given name Erh 耳. His birthplace was in the province of Honan 河南, approximately one hundred miles southwest from the birthplace of Confucius in the present-day province of Shantung 山東.

Lao Tzu is supposed to have been the keeper of the Royal Archives of the prefecture of Loyang 洛陽 when Confucius paid him a visit. After that visit Confucius said that Lao Tzu was like "a dragon soaring above the clouds."

During Lao Tzu's lifetime, the feudal states of the Chou dynasty were in disarray. Disgusted with the armed conflicts, senseless killings and the squandering of the country's wealth, Lao Tzu decided to withdraw from government service. He mounted a black ox and proceeded westward, intending to retire in the land beyond the frontier. There he felt he could develop his philosophy of Tao more completely. At the frontier pass, the officer in charge, named Kuan Yin-Tzu 關尹子, begged him to set down his philosophy before leaving the country. Lao Tzu agreed and spent the night in the guard house writing the *Tao-Te Ching* 道德經, or "Classic on the Way of Virtue," a short treatise consisting of about five thousand characters. The morning sun was just rising in the east as he finished his writing. He presented the treatise to Kuan, bade him fare-

Lao Tzu

well and continued his westward journey, never to be seen again.

The *Tao-Te Ching* is written in an enigmatic and poetic style, making it difficult to understand. Scholars to this day have differed in their interpretations, resulting in a considerable number of commentaries and many different translations. Some scholars question the authorship of the treatise, doubting that a man named Lao Tzu who was the keeper of the Royal Archives of Loyang ever existed. They also conjecture that the *Tao-Te Ching* was probably written or assembled in the third century B.C.

In discussing Taoism, a distinction must be made between the philosophy of Taoism and Taoism as the folk religion of China.

Philosophy of Taoism

The word *tao* literally means the "way," "road" or "path." Philosophically, the Tao is the cosmic "Way" that governs the operations of the universe. The philosophy of Taoism teaches one how to live in harmony with the Tao and the laws of the universe. In this way, wisdom is achieved and death is no longer anything to be feared.

Taoism maintains that the nature of the universe is beyond good and evil. Events occur regardless of human desires and human ethical standards. Those who try to construct codes of conduct and legislate righteousness only succeed in oppressing others with artificial rules and regulations. This interference with the laws of the universe, instead of improving things, only removes man further and further from the harmony implicit in the natural course of events. The wise man learns from the example of water, which flows around impediments and seeks the lowest level until at last it rejoins the sea.

The principal means of living in harmony with the universe was called *wu-wei* 無為, meaning "nonaction" or "nonstriving." This does not mean doing nothing; instead, it means refraining from attempts to force things and events to conform to one's desires and expectations. If one can be quiet within one's own mind and heart, one will be able to observe the world dispassionately and discern the natural flow of events. Staying in harmony with this flow brings wisdom and contentment. Life and death are seen as natural occurrences, just as the sun rises in the morning and sets in the evening only to rise again the following day. One allows the Tao to take its course without interference. Conflicts dissolve and one is imbued with an overflowing sense of peace.

It must be admitted that the philosophy of Taoism, although it had a great influence on Chinese artists and intellectuals, was never understood by the masses. The doctrine of non-striving made little sense to people who had to work from morning till evening just to provide for their daily needs of food and shelter. Only the few who had the time to read and reflect were able to understand it.

Taoism as Folk Religion

Taoism was also regarded as the core of the popular folk religion of China. Although there was little resemblance between the two, the followers of this religion claimed that they were practicing the teachings of Lao Tzu as recorded in the *Tao-Te Ching*.

The Taoist religion was animistic and heavily steeped with occult practices. Taoists worshipped everything in nature whether animate or inanimate. They believed that all things possessed a soul.

The first emperor of China, Chin Shih Huang Ti 秦始皇帝, gave the early Taoists a great boost when he dispatched a group of people to search for the "elixir" of immortality. This elixir was reported to be on an island somewhere in the Eastern Sea. The traditional account is that they failed in their mission and, fearing execution for their failure, decided to settle on the island rather than return to the emperor's court. This island in the Eastern Sea was said to be Japan, and the settlers in search of the elixir were thought to be the progenitors of the Japanese.

Some early Taoists were alchemists who devoted their efforts to transmuting base metals into gold and to finding the elusive elixir of immortality. Their experiments with compounds containing sulfur, arsenic, lead, zinc, copper, potassium, iron, charcoal and herbs paved the way for the discovery of dyes, gunpowder, porcelain, drugs and other products. Taoists, by experimenting with various herbs and medications, probably compiled the information contained in the first *Book on Herbs* 本草.

The founder of the present-day Taoist religion was generally considered to be Chang Tao-Ling 張道陵. According to legend, he was born on Heavenly Eye Mountain 天目山 in Chekiang 浙江 province in A.D. 35. At age seven, he mastered the arts of geomancy, astronomy and astrology. Lao Tzu himself was said to have descended from Heaven to teach Chang Tao-Ling the principles of Taoism. He then studied alchemy and attempted to find the elixir of immortality. After three years of research and with the help of the Blue Dragon and the White Tiger, he succeeded in discovering the secret of compounding the drug.

At age sixty, after taking the elixir, his face and body became those of a youth. He was the recipient of gifts from Heaven, including a mysterious book containing instructions for communicating with spirits, methods of self-transformation and the power to dispel evil spirits, goblins and devils. When a celestial messenger announced that Chang Tao-Ling had been given the knowledge to heal all types of illness, people flocked to him by the thousands. In exchange for treating the sick, he asked for five bushels of rice and thus was dubbed the "Rice Thief" 米賊.

Chang Tao-Ling died and ascended to Heaven at the age of 122. He kept the leader-

Chang Tao-Ling

ship of the Taoist religion within his own family by making the office a hereditary post. He left his heirs the mysterious book; a collection of charms, amulets and talismans; a magic sword and his official seal.

Chang Tao-Ling was usually depicted as an old man with a long beard riding on the back of a tiger. The title "Chang, the Master of Heaven" 張天師, more or less the equivalent of "Taoist pope," was conferred on the leader of the Taoist religion during the Tang 唐 dynasty (618–906). Around the year 1000, Chang Tao-Ling's heirs acquired Dragon-Tiger Mountain 龍虎山 in Kiangsi 江西 province, and the leaders of the Taoist religion have lived there ever since. One of the last leaders claimed that the uninterrupted succession had been continuous for sixty-three generations.

The Taoist pope ruled like a king over a motley group of Taoist priests 道士. His duty was mainly to confer honors and present gifts marked with the official seal of his office to visiting priests. The Taoist priests could be single or married. They derived their income by conducting ceremonies at the temple; selling incense, candles, paper offerings and charms; fortune telling; geomancy; conducting funeral ceremonies; communicating with the spirits of the dead and exorcising evil spirits. They usually did not preach or try to explain the philosophy of Taoism.

In Old China, Taoism and Buddhism borrowed extensively from each other and there were very few people who were strictly Taoist or strictly Buddhist. Thus the popular folk religion was largely a blend of the two beliefs.

Confucius

Confucius, the foremost sage of China, has been revered for centuries. Although little is known about his early life, historians believe that he lived from 551 to 479 B.C., although these dates are admittedly conjectural. His birthplace was a little village named Chueh-Li 闕里 in the feudal state of Lu 魯, located in present-day Shantung 山東 province.

At the time of his birth, his father, who was the mayor of the town, was rather old. His mother was much younger. One legend has it that his birth was heralded by a mythical unicorn that hovered over his home spitting out books 靈麟吐書. His given name was Kung Yau 孔丘 and his style name was Chung Ni 仲尼. Later he was recognized as Master Kung, or Kung Fu-Tzu 孔夫子. Westerners called him Confucius.

When his aged father died, Kung Yau was in his infancy. His mother raised him in poverty before remarrying and moving her family to the city of Chu Fu 曲阜. As a poor young man, Kung Yau earned his living by keeping accounts. He had little formal education but was self-taught and eventually became one of the most learned men of his time.

This was an age of great turmoil among the feudal states, with frequent conflict and bloodshed. Rulers were wicked and cruel, and officials taxed their subjects unmercifully. The oppressed people often suffered extreme poverty and starvation.

Confucius abhorred bad government. He made it his business to expound on good government and proper ethics. He eventually taught more than three thousand disciples, a remarkable number in those days. He instructed his students in the six arts of ceremonial rites, music, archery, chariot driving, writing and mathematics. There were no formal lectures. Discussions were held between individuals or in small groups.

Confucius taught that the state was an extension of the family. Political relationships were like parent-child relationships. He said, "When those in high positions perform well their duties to their relatives, all the people will be aroused to virtue." He believed in maintaining the ancient rituals and proper ceremonies. If the ruling class set a good example, the country as a whole would be at peace and would prosper. He also believed in social justice and sought to eliminate inequities.

Regarding proper ethics, he believed that if every individual knew his exact position in relationship to others and also knew the particular rights and responsibilities attached to that position, peace within the social order would prevail. He established a three-level hierarchy of subordination: the subordination of the young to the elders, the female to the male and the people to the established authority. He taught the principles of the Five Human Relationships—those between ruler and subject, father and son, husband and wife, elder brother and younger brother, and friend and friend.

In the family system, he placed a premium on seniority. The apex of the structure was the oldest living male, who was the leader of the family in all respects. He possessed absolute authority and his commands had to be completely obeyed by his subordinates. At the same time, it was assumed that with old age came the wisdom gained in long experience. The head of the family was expected to rule benevolently and justly. Filial piety was considered the supreme virtue in the family. Proper rituals in mourning and burial as well as honor-

Confucius

ing the ancestral spirits were all stressed because they were an extension of filial piety.

Confucius wanted to cultivate the Perfect Man 君子. In his middle age, often accompanied by his disciples, he traveled from state to state trying to persuade the rulers to govern with virtue and justice. He advocated avoiding war, reducing taxes and eliminating abuse of power and corruption. The rulers of Lu and other feudal states thought that Confucius' ideas were radical and dangerous. His enemies charged that he was a political schemer and an opportunist, sowing seeds of discord to gain power for himself.

In his private life, Confucius was a frustrated and unhappy man. He lacked a sense of humor and displayed little love for children. Except for his mother, he had little regard for women. He divorced his wife, who apparently was a nasty, ill-tempered woman. His only son died before him.

Late in life, Confucius gave up his travels and resettled in Lu, where he continued to teach. He said, "I am a man descended from the royal house of Yin, but I see no sovereign in the empire who will take my advice. My time has come to die." He died in 479 B.C., at the age of seventy-three, in relative obscurity and with a sense of failure. He was survived by a grandson, Tzu Szu 子思.

Many years after his death, Confucius was recognized as a sage, a great teacher and a political reformer. His ideas exerted a powerful influence not only in China but also in Korea, Japan, and Southeast Asia. Societies and temples were established throughout China to honor him. Even the Taoists deified Confucius, believing that he caused literature to flourish and the world to prosper.

Memorial services for Confucius were held twice a year at the spring and autumn equinoxes. These services varied greatly. Some were very simple. The most elaborate were the formal national rites held in Peking. This ceremony started at 3:00 a.m. in the main Confucian temple. All the officials were properly robed, and an atmosphere of solemnity prevailed. Ancient musical instruments such as jade chimes, bells, gongs and drums added to the solemnity of the occasion. Incense was burned and offerings were made of pigs, sheep, calves, grains, fruits, oils and wine.

People frequently ask, "Is Confucianism a religion?" The answer of course depends on one's definition of a religion. Some have claimed that Confucianism is not a religion. Confucius emphasized ethical behavior and saw man primarily as a social being defined by a nexus of human relationships. He had little to say about God, the supernatural or the life hereafter, preferring to remain agnostic on those questions. However, he did stress the importance of a proper attitude toward the dead in the rituals of mourning and burial and believed in honoring the ancestral spirits. For these reasons, it is possible to maintain that Confucianism does encompass some of the concerns that are usually regarded as religious.

Mencius

The second great sage of China was Meng Tzu 孟子, meaning "Master Meng." Like that of Kung Fu-Tzu, this name was anglicized to Mencius. Little is known about his early life, although it is believed that he was born in the state of Tsou 鄒, in the present-day province of Shantung, and lived from 372 to 289 B.C., about one hundred years after the death of Confucius. He lost his father at the age of three and was raised by his mother. Countless numbers of children in China have heard the story about "Mencius' Mother's Three Moves" 孟母三遷.

These moves were attempts to expose Mencius to a good environment. On her first move, she located her family outside the city. As it happened, their house was near a cemetery. There Mencius observed the grave diggers, the chanting priests, the wailing mourners and numerous burials. For recreation, Mencius and his playmates began imitating the rites of burial. Seeing this, his mother decided to move to the business section of the city. Here she noticed her son mimicking the peddlers and hawkers who yelled and haggled over their goods and wares. She concluded that this atmosphere was also having an adverse effect on her son, so she chose to move again to another location. This third move settled the family next to a school. Here, to her delight, she found that the students, teachers and scholars provided the perfect environment for her son. Little Mencius was soon imitating these learned people. They were serious, upright in their behavior and cultured. They studied and performed the proper rites, and were excellent role models for her impressionable young son.

One day, while his mother was weaving at her loom, Mencius returned home instead of attending classes. When asked why he had come home, he gave no reason. His mother seized a knife and slashed the cloth on the loom, admonishing him, "If you stay away from school for no good reason, you will be like this cloth, useless."

Later, after he had married, Mencius entered his bedchamber unannounced one day and found his wife changing her clothes. He

Mencius

scolded his wife for her uncouth behavior. His mother told him, "You were wrong and you should be reprimanded. It is said in the *Record of Rites* 禮記, 'Before entering through the door of a parlor or a private chamber, announce your presence.'"

After studying with a Confucian scholar, Mencius became a zealous supporter of Confucian precepts. Like Confucius, he traveled to the feudal states and lectured to the rulers and princes, trying to convince them to reform their governments. Although he was received with courtesy and respect, his ideas for reform were no more successful than Confucius' had been. They were still regarded as radical and dangerous.

After forty years of travel and frustration, Mencius decided to retire. With the help of his disciples, he turned to editing some of the classic texts of Confucianism, adding his own *Discourses of Mencius* 孟子書 to the corpus.

Mencius maintained that government should

be benevolent. In governing, a wise ruler holds the welfare of the people foremost, the interest of the state second and his own interest last. Like Confucius, he thought that only good and virtuous men should rule. The state should promote the material welfare of its citizens by providing them with adequate food and clothing. Bad rulers who demonstrated neither benevolence nor concern for the welfare of the people should be corrected. If that proved impossible, they could be overthrown by rebellion, for in their intransigence they would have lost the Mandate of Heaven to rule. He proposed the establishment of schools and the spread of literacy. He promoted agriculture and advocated the equal distribution of wealth, the protection of the weak and the old and the reduction of taxes. He favored the restoration of the Nine-Square System 井田, according to which eight families cultivated the nine squares. Each family was allotted one square at the periphery, with the center square being jointly cultivated by the eight families for the state.

Although Mencius was honored as a great sage in China, special memorial services for him never became an annual tradition. Mencius' spiritual tablet was usually placed in Confucian temples, although there were also a few temples that were solely dedicated to him. At Sheldrake village 鳧村 in Shantung province, where his mother was born and finally settled, a shrine was built and a stone tablet erected to commemorate her "Three Moves."

CHAPTER 8

Traditional Chinese Medicine

Bounded by the cold barren tundra in the north, the wide expanse of the Pacific Ocean in the east, the thick dense jungles to the south and the high imposing mountains of the Himalayas in the west, China remained almost completely isolated from the rest of the world for centuries. Because of this isolation, the Chinese developed a distinctive system of medicine that has dominated medical thinking in China right up to the present day. This unique system has also influenced the medical concepts of Korea, Japan and parts of Southeast Asia.

Fundamental to traditional Chinese medicine is the philosophy built on the concepts of Tao 道, yin 陰 and yang 陽, and the Five Elements 五行. Tao literally means the "road" or "way," but philosophically it signifies the cosmic Way or the harmony between Heaven and Earth and between this world and the world beyond. To follow the Tao is to be in accord with the fundamental laws of the universe.

The symbol of yin and yang is a circle divided by an S-shaped line into areas of dark and light, representing the basic dualism of the universe. Everything, regardless of whether it is concrete or abstract, physical or moral, can be classified as yin or yang. Yin is the passive or negative principle, and it includes the female, the moon, earth, water, darkness, evil, poverty and sadness. In contrast, yang is the active or positive principle, and it includes the male, the sun, heaven, fire, brightness, good, wealth and joy. Yin and yang were not regarded as conflicting principles but as complementary forces. The universe depends on the interaction of yin and yang. As the symbol indicates, each penetrates the other's hemisphere and together they are resolved in an all-embracing circle, the symbol of Tao.

Intimately associated with yin and yang are

Yin and yang in the Tao, the all-embracing circle

the Five Elements. It was believed that all things are composed of five elements: metal 金, wood 木, water 水, fire 火 and earth 土. The proportions of these elements are determined by the mutual influence of yin and yang.

Chinese concepts of health and disease are closely related to this cosmogony. Out of chaos comes the Tao, which produces the two cosmic forces of yin and yang. The compounding of yin and yang produces the Five Elements. Since man and the universe have been created from the same identical elements, man is subject to the same forces that govern the universe. If man remains in harmony with the Tao, and yin and yang and the Five Elements are in proper balance, he can enjoy good health and longevity. Imbalance, however, results in illness and death.

With these concepts of health and disease, the basic physical sciences of anatomy, chemistry, physiology, bacteriology and pathology, all of which were essential to the development of Western medicine, are practically nonexistent in traditional Chinese medicine. Although the Chinese had a fairly good knowledge of surface anatomy, their understanding of gross and microscopic anatomy was either lacking or rudimentary and inaccurate. They believed that there are 12 channels or main ducts, not blood vessels, corresponding to the 12 months of a year and carrying vital air and blood through the body. These channels, which were believed to be embedded deep in the muscles, emerge at 365 points on the skin surface. The 365 points, of course, correspond to the days of a year. The human body was also believed to consist of 365 parts—including the five viscera 五臟, the heart, spleen, lungs, liver and kidneys, corresponding to the Five Elements; and the six bowels 六腑, the stomach,

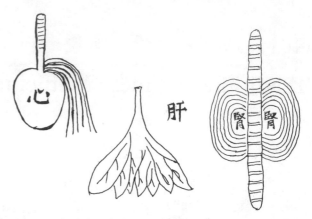

Anatomical drawings of the heart, liver and kidneys

small intestines, large intestines, gallbladder, urinary bladder and the "three burning spaces" 三焦.

Old Chinese anatomical drawings of the human body and its organs are crude and incorrect. Only two cases of human dissection were recorded in Chinese literature up to A.D. 1160. This was because the Chinese believed that the human body given by one's ancestors was sacred and must not be violated even after death. This belief explains, to a degree, the traditional aversion to surgical operations and autopsies.

Chinese physiology considers the five viscera to be the main organs, used primarily for storage. The functions of the six bowels all relate to elimination. The organs serve as officials of a nation. For example, the heart serves as a minister who excels in insight and understanding; the liver serves as a minister who excels in strategic planning; the kidneys are officials who do energetic work; the stomach acts as the controller of public granaries; the large intestines are officials who propagate the right way of living and the "three burning spaces" are officials who plan the ditches, sluices and waterways.

The basis of traditional Chinese medicine is an ancient text known as the Yellow Emperor's *Classic of Internal Medicine* 黃帝內經. Although it was attributed to Huang Ti 黃帝, the legendary Yellow Emperor who reigned from 2698 to 2598 B.C., it is doubtful that he wrote it. The core text was probably written many centuries later and was gradually expanded by subsequent authors. Research has so far failed to discover a definite date or the name of the original author of this classic.

Diagnosis and Treatment

In traditional Chinese medicine, four methods may be employed to make a medical diagnosis. The physician looks, listens, inquires and feels the pulse. Feeling the pulse is considered the best method, and often is the only method used in diagnosis.

Palpation of the pulse is a complicated procedure that can last anywhere from ten minutes to several hours. Each radial pulse, or pulse at the wrist, is divided into three sections. Beginning with the wrist and progressing upward toward the elbow, the sections of the radial pulse are called the "inch" 寸, the "bar" or "pass" 關 and the "cubit" 尺. Each section is further subdivided into a deep and a superficial pulse. Thus, for two wrists, there are a total of twelve pulses. Each pulse is believed to be connected to a specific organ, and thus it can reflect the fluctuations of yin and yang and the pathological changes of the organ. The pulses are influenced by many factors including age, sex, stature, temperament, time of day, season of the year and positions of the constellations.

Examination of the pulse reveals not only the location and nature of the illness but also its likely outcome.

The description of the various pulses in the traditional literature is often vague and ambiguous. There are supposed to be four basic pulses—deep, superficial, slow and quick. A deep pulse is like a stone thrown in water, while a superficial pulse is like wood floating on water. A slow pulse is considered to be three beats to one respiratory cycle of inspiration and expiration. A quick pulse is six or more beats to one respiratory cycle. In addition, pulses are described as ascending, descending, coming and returning. There is a pulse like the pecking of a bird and one as hollow as an onion stalk. Some pulses are like the rolling of thunder, others are like pebbles rolling in a basin. There is even one as light as the rustle of falling leaves.

The person examining the patient's pulse must be in perfect tranquility. The best time to examine the pulse was thought to be sunrise. A ratio of four pulse beats of the patient to one cycle of inspiration and expiration of the examiner is considered to be normal and healthy. If the pulse beats fifty times without interruption, it is a sign of good health. If the pulse stops after forty beats, one of the five major organs must be diseased and the patient is seldom given longer than five years to live. If the pulse stops after thirty beats, death is expected within three years. If the pulse flutters after two beats, death is imminent and expected within two to three days.

Diseases are thought to be caused by both internal and external factors. Internal factors include anger, hate, jealousy, grief and fright. Typical external factors are dryness, dampness, heat, cold and drafts. The primary aim in treatment is to restore the balance of yin and yang. Traditional methods of treatment include curing the spirits, medication (especially with herbs), massage, simple manipulations, acupuncture and moxibustion.

The Chinese Pharmacopia

The Chinese pharmacopia was very extensive. A *Catalog of Native Herbs* 本草綱目, written by Li Shih-Chen 李時珍 and completed after his death by his son, is a traditional Chinese materia medica. Over a period of twenty years, the two authors consulted every known publication on the subject, completing their research in 1578. Their catalog was presented to Emperor Wan Li 萬歷 of the Ming 明 dynasty, who authorized its publication in 1596. This classic is regarded as the most comprehensive and authoritative work on the subject up to the present day.

An encyclopedia in 52 volumes, the *Catalog of Native Herbs* discusses 1,892 drugs and contains 8,160 prescriptions. This exhaustive treatise includes not only native herbs but also drugs derived from metal, stones, garments, utensils, insects, fish and mollusks. It also includes drugs derived from reptiles, birds, animals and parts of the human body—in fact, practically anything imaginable, even mythical birds and beasts.

The catalog of drugs that Li Shih-Chen codified was developed empirically over the course of centuries—that is, through trial and error, various beneficial and poisonous substances were discovered and recorded. There was no scientific research or animal experimentation. Moreover, no distinction was made between food and drugs. Foods in general were classified as dehydrating 熱, cooling 涼, nourishing 補 and deleterious 毒. The same factors were also considered in the treatment of diseases.

The shapes and colors of medications were given careful consideration. Roots, herbs and drugs of certain shapes or colors were thought to be beneficial in the treatment of the organ or the disease which they happened to resemble. For example, pig's liver was used to treat the accumulation of fluid within the abdominal cavity caused by weakness of the human liver. Yellow saffron was used to treat yellow jaundice. Homonyms were also a factor in the selection of medications, which could be either avoided or prescribed on that basis. For example, beans, or *tou* 豆, were avoided by patients afflicted with chickenpox, or *tou* 痘, since it was believed that ingestion of beans aggravated chickenpox.

Chinese herbs and medications are well known for often producing good results and such medications are probably based on sound pharmacological principles. Some of these same medications were also discovered in Western medicine, including iodine from seaweeds, ephedrine from the native herb *ma huang* 麻黃, calcium from the velvet of deer horn 鹿茸 and *kaolin* 高嶺土, a fine clay used in diarrhea drugs. At the same time, Chinese physicians have prescribed some strange and exotic drugs which may or may not have any medicinal value—for example, ginseng, angelica root, dried sea horse, dried red-spotted lizard, snake, gallbladder of the bear, tiger bone, rhinoceros horn and the exuviae of the cicada.

Ginseng 人參, the Chinese drug par excellence, was prescribed as a panacea when all other drugs failed. A sweet aromatic root with a trace of bitterness, ginseng was used to strengthen the five viscera, brighten the eyes,

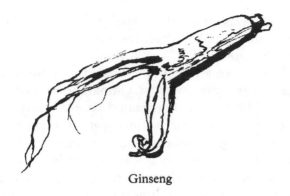

Ginseng

Angelica root

allay fears, promote understanding and lower fevers. It was also used to stop hemorrhages, counteract debility and prolong life. It was used to treat every type of disease and was given without fear of harmful side effects. Curiously, ginseng has been analyzed and found to possess no important pharmacological properties.

The Chinese have always been willing to pay exorbitant prices for good ginseng. The best ginseng was the wild ginseng 野人參 from Manchuria, now practically extinct. At one time, it was reserved solely for the emperor and his household. The next best ginseng are those varieties cultivated in Korea and Manchuria. Japanese, American and Canadian varieties are considered relatively inferior.

Angelica root or *tang kuei* 當歸 was frequently used and highly prized as a drug for women. The fleshy brown root is divided into many rootlets. The cut surface is soft and either white or yellowish in color. The taste of the root is bittersweet and the strong odor resembles that of celery. Angelica root was used to treat menstrual disorders, chlorotic anemia and hemorrhagic conditions of all types occurring in women. *Tang kuei* literally means "ought to return home," alluding to the notion

that after a woman has taken the drug she should return home to her husband, because it was considered to be a potent aphrodisiac.

Dried sea horse 海馬 was used to treat tumors of the neck and to loosen phlegm. Dried gecko 蛤蚧, the large red-spotted lizard, was used as a tonic for people with asthma, tuberculosis and neurasthenia, a nervous condition characterized by fatigue and anxiety. In addition, it was used to improve vigor and sexual potency in men.

Snake 蛇 was used to treat diseases caused by winds and dampness 風濕. The viper 白花蛇 was used to treat syphilis and worm infestation. The gallbladder of the bear 熊膽 and tiger bone 虎骨 were both believed to be good for aches and pains, while rhinoceros horn 犀角

Dried sea horse and gecko

Exuviae of the cicada

was used to expel fevers and anxiety and to treat convulsions in children and infants.

The exuviae of the cicada 蟬蛻, the cast-off coverings of the insect after molting, were used for headaches, colds and convulsions. It was claimed that when they were cooked with pig's liver and eaten, they helped to strengthen weak eyesight in older people.

Acupuncture, Moxibustion and Other Treatments

Acupuncture 針灸, an ancient Chinese method of treatment, has supposedly been practiced for four thousand years. It consists of inserting needles—made of gold, silver, copper, iron and other metals—into the body at specific points. Acupuncture needles can be fine or coarse and they vary in length from 3 to 24 centimeters. There are 365 acupuncture points, marking the spots where the 12 channels emerge at the skin surface. It was believed that needling the appropriate points helps to restore the proper balance of yin and yang in the diseased organ. For example, to treat acute appendicitis, a needle is inserted at a point below the right knee to stimulate the healing of the inflamed appendix.

Moxibustion 艾火, a technique of burning mugwort leaves 艾草 on the skin, was often used in conjunction with acupuncture. Moxi-

bustion was applied to the site of the acupuncture, usually after the needle had been withdrawn.

Aside from a few minor procedures, surgery was never developed in China. Some traditional Chinese doctors treated simple fractures by aligning the bone, splinting it with bamboo and applying medication on the skin over the fracture site to promote healing. Others treated entropion, a condition where the edge of the eyelid grows inward toward the eyeball, by

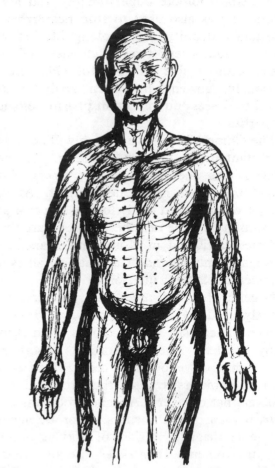

Hollow copper acupuncture mannequin (Sung period)

clamping the eyelid with bamboo sticks and letting the edge slough off.

Castration was the only surgical operation of any magnitude, and it was practiced from 1000 B.C. up to the twentieth century. Originally a form of punishment, it was later used to provide eunuchs for the imperial household, especially male servants for the women's quarters. This crude operation was carried out by removing the external male sex organs with a single stroke of a sickle-shaped knife. The urethra was then plugged with pewter, and hemorrhage was controlled with tight bandages. Hemorrhage, infection and urinary incontinence were the chief complications. The period of convalescence was usually quite long, and the mortality rate was approximately two percent for this operation.

In the field of obstetrics and gynecology, traditional doctors diagnosed, advised and prescribed. Pelvic examination and delivery were left strictly to older women and midwives.

Gods of Medicine

Traditional Chinese medicine was similar in many ways to Western medicine up to the time of the Renaissance and Reformation. Thereafter, Western medicine forged ahead while traditional Chinese medicine remained at a standstill. Many reasons have been proposed for this stagnation. For one thing, there was no tradition of scientific research. Scholars devoted their time chiefly to literature, history, government, ethics and philosophy. A scholar endangered his reputation if he exerted himself physically or soiled his hands. The natural sciences, including medicine, lay beyond the scholar's proper scope and interests. More-over, among those who did become medical practitioners, there was no sense of cumulative development. Medical discoveries were made haphazardly and were not publicized; indeed, they were often deliberately kept secret. The Chinese have always had an unusual reverence for the traditional learning embodied in the various classics. While there is something admirable in this attitude, adherence to mistaken beliefs stifled Chinese advancement in science just as blind adherence to the teachings of Aristotle hampered Western scientific progress for many centuries.

Before turning to the supernatural remedies that the Chinese resorted to in times of illness, it is instructive to consider the magnitude of the health care problem in old China. Millions of people needed medical attention daily, and this huge population was plagued with every type of disease. People were poor, especially the peasants who constituted over 80 percent of the population, and frequently on the brink of starvation. Diseases such as measles, chicken-pox, smallpox, whooping cough, diphtheria, tetanus, typhoid and cholera killed millions annually. Other killers were malnutrition, intestinal diseases, venereal diseases, tuberculosis, leprosy, malaria, parasitic infestations, high blood pressure and heart diseases. Still other killers were diabetes, cancer and opium addiction. In addition, deaths of mothers in childbirth were appallingly high. Women died from childbed fever, hemorrhage and convulsions. Women had no care during pregnancy and were delivered by untrained women or midwives. Every fifth child died before attaining his first birthday.

Illiteracy was widespread and the people knew nothing of simple hygiene, basic sanitation or elementary science. They were superstitious and believed that illnesses were caused by demons and evil spirits. Consequently, health care was woefully inadequate. Before the late 1800s, only traditional Chinese medicine was practiced. Even then, the number of practitioners was insufficient. The abilities of these doctors varied considerably. Some were graduates of traditional Chinese medical schools. Many were charlatans who perused medical books, acquired a reputation as a doctor and treated patients. Others dispensed medical care because they had in their possession secret prescriptions. Traditional Chinese doctors had no knowledge of surgery. There were no hospitals for the sick, and dental care was nonexistent. The doctors with superior training avoided small villages and practiced in large cities where the affluent were able to afford their services. It is not surprising that life expectancy in old China was very low, below thirty years of age.

In these conditions, the Chinese relied on their gods and goddesses for the prevention and treatment of diseases. They depended on prayers, incantations, charms, amulets, temple prescriptions and ceremonies to exorcise or placate the spirits causing illnesses.

Yao Wang

Among the host of gods and goddesses whom the Chinese depended on at times of illness, one of the most popular was the King of Remedies, Yao Wang 藥王. It was believed that the King of Remedies had originally been a mortal named Sun Ssu-Miao 孫思邈, a native of Shensi 陝西 province. He was extremely intelligent at a very early age. It was said that in his youth, he was able to learn one thousand written characters a day.

After the ruler Hsuan Wang 宣王 (827–721 B.C.) defeated the barbarians from the north, Sun became a hermit at Tai-Po Shan 太白山. Here he met Chiu Chen-Jen 仇眞人, who taught him the secrets of yin and yang and the science of immortality.

On one of his journeys, Sun met a shepherd who was trying to kill a snake. He saved the snake by giving his robe to the shepherd and imploring him to spare the snake. Sun then carefully treated the injured snake and allowed it to slither away. Ten days later, he encountered a horseman who dismounted and cordially invited Sun to meet his father and receive his thanks. He accepted the invitation and was presented to a dignified, polite and gracious gentleman, the Dragon King 龍王.

The Dragon King brought out his infant son dressed in blue and told Sun that his son had wandered out to play one day and was almost killed by a shepherd. He thanked Sun for giving his robe to the shepherd and for nursing his son's wound and allowing him to return home. With deep gratitude, he presented Sun with a book entitled *Secrets of the Dragon* 龍藏, which contained thirty chapters of marvelous prescriptions that were beneficial to mankind. These prescriptions were later incorporated into Sun's book, *The Thousand Golden Prescriptions* 千金簡易方.

Sun was reported to have cured Emperor Kao Tsung 高宗 (650–684) of the Tang 唐 dynasty, who was afflicted with severe headaches. He also successfully treated the emperor's intestinal infection, which had been giving him abdominal pain, fever and diarrhea, by strengthening the emperor's stomach and kidneys.

When Sun Ssu-Miao died in 682, his corpse remained perfectly preserved and did not decay or putrefy for a whole month. At the time of burial, when his body was about to be placed in the coffin, the corpse mysteriously disappeared, leaving only Sun's clothing behind.

Sun was later deified as the King of Remedies, Yao Wang. He was usually depicted with two attendants, one carrying a gourd filled with magic pills and drugs, the other holding a leaf from a medicinal herb.

Hua To

Hua To 華陀 (A.D. 136–220), the celebrated surgeon and patron deity of surgeons, was next to Yao Wang in popularity. A native of Anhui 安徽 province, Hua To lived during the period of disintegration of the Han 漢 dynasty.

By studying medicine under the famous doctor Yang Li-Kung 陽勵公, Hua To became a skillful diagnostician as well as an expert in acupuncture and cauterization. According to legend, he had no hesitation to resort to surgery when other methods failed. He would administer an oral anesthetic, thought to be hashish, and proceed to suture wounds, remove stones from various organs, excise diseased tissues and resect parts of the intestines and grafted organs. He was also skilled in chest, orthopedic, nasal and brain surgery. After the surgical operation, he would apply medication to the injured parts. Healing usually followed and the patient's health was restored.

In a popular legend, Hua To is summoned to remove a poisoned arrow lodged deep in the upper arm of Kuan Ti 關帝, the God of War. When he offers the warrior an anesthetic drug to deaden the pain, the brave and stoic Kuan Ti absolutely refuses it. Hua To then incises the soft tissues, removes the arrow and scrapes the bone clean while Kuan Ti nonchalantly continues his chess game with Ma Liang 馬良.

Hua To

The famous surgeon was also summoned by Tsao Tsao 曹操, pretender to the throne of the kingdom of Wei 魏, to treat his intractable headaches. Hua To suggested cutting a hole in the skull to release the noxious humor causing the headaches. Thinking that it was a ruse to murder him, Tsao Tsao imprisoned Hua To and condemned him to death.

While imprisoned, Hua To gave his books on medicine and surgery to one of the jailers who was kind to him. Unfortunately the wife of this jailer, fearing the gift might implicate her husband, burned the priceless books. The only volume not destroyed was one dealing with veterinary medicine. As a result, the Chinese lost all their knowledge in the art of surgery.

Realizing that his execution was imminent, Hua To committed suicide by drinking poison. For more than a year after his burial, smoke continued to rise from his tomb.

Goddesses of Medicine

A popular god of medicine in southern China was the Goddess of the Golden Flower 金花娘娘. This relatively new goddess was worshipped as the guardian of women and children.

Originally a native of the city of Canton 廣州, she is said to have lived during the reign of Emperor Cheng Hua 成花 (1465–1487) of the Ming 明 dynasty. According to legend, she was extremely devoted to religion in her youth and regularly visited all the temples in her neighborhood. Moreover, she was endowed with the ability to communicate with the spirits of the dead.

Disgusted with the evil in the world, she eventually drowned herself in a river. When her corpse surfaced and was taken out of the water, the air was filled with fragrant odors. When the body was placed in a coffin, an idol of Golden Flower rose from the river and remained stationary in the air. The awe-stricken populace proclaimed her to be a goddess and built a temple to house the idol.

Women who were barren or pregnant and women with sick children prayed to her for help. She had many responsibilities and was aided by many assistants. Each assistant was assigned a specific duty. The assistants helped barren women to conceive, protected pregnant women so that they would deliver safely, and blessed women so that they would deliver sons. The assistants also protected unborn children, supervised the cutting of the umbilical cord, supervised the feeding of infants and children and taught them to suckle and nurse. They also attended to the preparation of an infant's food, made children smile, made them happy and taught them to walk and speak. They guarded children from smallpox, prevented their bodies from developing sores and gave them good health and strength.

Thus, certain deities can be seen to have been way ahead of their time in having specialists and subspecialists in the field of medicine. Some of the noteworthy specialists are the following:

The Goddess of Vision 眼光菩薩 helped to prevent and cure eye diseases that caused blindness. She was depicted holding an eye in her hands. The Hastener of Childbirth 催生娘娘 was the goddess who hastened delivery. Women prayed to her for help and protection during labor and delivery. The Lady for Pregnant Women 大奶娘娘 assisted in making childbirth easy, painless and safe.

Ko Ku 葛姑 was the Goddess of Midwives. This deity, a native of Anhui province, had originally been a famous and skillful midwife. Her deification was relatively recent, occurring during the reign of Emperor Kuang Hsu 光緒 (1875–1909) of the Ching 清 dynasty.

The Goddess of Smallpox 痘神娘娘 cared for people afflicted with smallpox. This Taoist goddess was depicted with a shawl protecting her from the cold. She supervised several assistants: the Spirit of Blackpox 癍神, who protected people when the smallpox reached the grayish or dangerous stage; the Spirit of Scarlet Fever 痧神, who watched over children with this common infectious disease, and the Spirit of Pockmarks 麻神, who prevented disfigurement from smallpox.

In addition to seeking help from the gods of medicine, people frequently prayed to other gods and goddesses in times of illness. Some of these were the Goddess of Mercy, Kuan Yin 觀音; the God of War, Kuan Ti 關帝; the local Earth God, Tu Ti 土地, and the Buddha of Healing, Yao-Shih Fo 藥師佛. Besides praying to these deities for help, people often presented packets of tea leaves to them for blessing. The tea leaves were mingled with ashes from the incense sticks at the temple altar. When steeped and drunk, this spiritual tea 神茶 was believed to be beneficial.

CHAPTER 9

Marriage, Birth and Death

Marriage, the birth of children and the celebration of birthdays are all milestones in the life of an individual. In old China these events were considered formal occasions and were observed with specific rites and ceremonies. So also was the case with death, which was observed with appropriate solemnity.

Marriage Customs

Marriage was an extremely important event in a Chinese family. Parents wanted their sons to marry well and produce grandsons so that the family would be perpetuated and the ancestral spirits would be worshipped without interruption. To produce no sons after marriage was considered a major breach of filial piety.

Because marriage was so significant, the choice of partners was not left to the bride and groom, who had little or no say in the matter. Arrangements for the betrothal and marriage were initiated by the father, by an older brother or by an influential close relative. The families negotiated through a go-between or matchmaker 媒人, and the contract agreed upon by the two families was binding. It was not uncommon for the bride and groom to meet each other for the first time on the day of the wedding.

When a son reached the age of sixteen, his father sought the services of a matchmaker, usually a woman, who would seek to arrange a marriage with another family of equal rank, social standing and wealth. She also tried to select a mate who would be compatible. People with incurable diseases such as leprosy or insanity, people with serious deformities, people whose family members had committed grave and heinous crimes or who were theatrical performers, slaves or outcasts such as the boat people 蛋家 were excluded. These people married among themselves. There were also other customs prohibiting many types of marriages. Girls younger than fourteen were forbidden to marry. Marriages were not permitted between persons with the same surname because they were considered relatives. The punishment for violating this prohibition was sixty lashes and annulment of the marriage. A man was forbidden to marry the daughter of his father's sister, the daughter of his mother's sister or the sister of his mother. Punishment for any such violation was death by strangulation.

Marriages occurred throughout the year. The most propitious time, however, was from the fifteenth day of the eighth moon to the fourth moon. During the ninth moon, which was regarded as unfavorable, marriages did not take place except in cases of extreme urgency, such as the impending death of a parent of the involved parties. Marriages were postponed when either family was in mourning.

Betrothal and marriage customs varied in different parts of the country. They varied from village to village even when the villages were in close proximity.

Usually, after the matchmaker selected a suitable girl for the groom, there were six betrothal ceremonies and five marriage rituals that were performed on auspicious days. These were highly detailed ceremonies, which included notification to various gods and to the spirits of the departed ancestors, who were asked for their blessings. The first betrothal ceremony was performed about six weeks prior to the wedding. In this ceremony, the families of the prospective bride and groom exchanged information. The father of the young man furnished the father of the young lady with his son's "eight characters" 八字, which specified the hour, the day and the year of his birth. He received a similar document from the young lady's father. After receiving the eight characters, each side consulted an astrologer who would cast the horoscopes of the prospective bride and groom. If it was determined that the marriage would be successful and happy, the betrothal ceremonies continued.

The next ceremony was the offer of marriage. The father of the young man wrote a formal letter to the father of the young lady stating his wish that she become the wife of his son. On an auspicious day, the matchmaker—

"Double Happiness" character

either alone or accompanied by a friend of the prospective groom's family—delivered the letter together with cakes and other gifts to the family of the girl. The cakes were contained in large red lacquer boxes. On the lid of each box was a broad strip of red paper inscribed with the character for "double happiness" 囍 in gold ink.

The third ceremony was the acceptance of the marriage proposal. The father of the girl replied by writing a letter of consent and approval. This letter, properly addressed to the father of the young man, was sealed and placed in a small box. The boxes containing the cakes from the prospective groom's family were returned with some of the cakes. The small box with the letter of reply and the cake boxes were presented to the matchmaker for delivery.

An exchange of gifts constituted the fourth ceremony, performed approximately two and a half weeks prior to the wedding. Gifts that had previously been negotiated and agreed upon were sent to the bride-elect and her family. These gifts included wedding cakes in lacquer boxes properly labeled with the character for "double happiness," exotic foods, sweetmeats, wine, expensive tea, gold coins, hairpins, earrings, bracelets, beads, silk, bridal clothes and a whole roast pig. The family of the bride-elect returned the cake boxes with some of the cakes. They presented their selection of foods, wine and teas, and gave linens to their daughter's future mother-in-law. Parts of the roast pig—including the head and hind portion with trotters, symbolizing that with every undertaking in life there was a beginning and an end—were also returned. In addition, the bride-elect's family gave the prospective groom a formal robe and a money bag stuffed with coins.

The cakes received by the families were distributed to relatives and friends and served as announcements of the impending marriage. After the exchange of gifts, the marriage could not be annulled except under very unusual circumstances. People congratulated the prospective groom's parents for "acquiring a daughter-in-law" and the parents of the bride-elect for "marrying off a daughter."

The fifth ceremony was the selection of the wedding date. The father of the prospective groom, after consulting with an astrologer, selected an auspicious day. The matchmaker then delivered to the other family a letter designating the day of the wedding. But before presenting it to the father of the bride-elect, the matchmaker courteously asked the girl's father to select the wedding date. He politely declined the honor and said the boy's father should decide. The letter designating the wedding date was then presented.

For about two weeks prior to the wedding, the bride-elect remained in seclusion with her sisters, girlfriends and attendants. They expressed deep sorrow because she was leaving the family. Manuals were given to her so that she could prepare herself for the duties and responsibilities of marriage. Eventually these manuals would be passed on to a favorite friend preparing for her own marriage.

On an auspicious day, either before the wedding or on the day of the wedding, the bride-elect's trousseau, bedding, furniture and personal belongings were sent to her future home.

On the day of her marriage, the bride was given a ceremonial bath with water purified with pomelo leaves. She was dressed in her finest, and her hair was styled in a coiffure signifying her new status as a married woman. Her face was made up with cosmetics, but no rouge was applied. A coronet decorated with strings of dangling pearls was placed on her head. A red silk veil was placed over her face to shield her from untoward glances. A small mirror was hung from her neck to ward off evil spirits. She carried a folding fan in her hand.

The sixth and final betrothal ceremony was performed before she left her home. At the family altar, she honored the gods and the spirits of her ancestors, and before leaving home, she served tea with sweetmeats and reverently bowed to her parents and elders.

The five rituals of marriage followed. The first was the procession of the bride to her future home; this usually took place in the early evening. The bride was carefully helped into the red sedan-chair which she would never again ride in after the wedding. The heavy sedan-chair was ornamented with carvings and kingfisher feathers. Accompanied by musicians, men carrying banners, lantern bearers, gong beaters, the matchmaker and her attendants, she then proceeded to her future home. Firecrackers were burned to signify the happy event.

The bride's parents usually did not attend the wedding. They remained at home in their everyday clothes. A small dinner might be hosted for close relatives and friends.

The second ritual commenced when the bride arrived at the home of the groom. Upon arrival, she was greeted with the burning of firecrackers. She was helped from the red sedan-chair, placed on the back of a female servant and then carefully carried over a small fire for purification. After that, she was escorted into the family hall.

The third and fourth rituals were conducted at the altar in the family hall. At the newly refurbished altar were incense, candles and offerings of food, tea and wine. Here the groom unveiled his bride and saw her face for the first time. Together, the bride and groom worshipped Heaven and Earth, the household gods and the spirits of his ancestors. The couple then drank a little wine served in two little porcelain cups tied together with a red cord. This, the wedding ceremony, was concluded with the burning of a string of firecrackers.

The newly wedded couple was then led into the bedroom, where they prayed to the Duke of the Bed 牀公 and the Lady of the Bed 牀婆. These two spirits protected the occupants of the bed and blessed them with many sons.

The couple then returned to the family hall, where the fifth and last marriage ritual was held. This was the tea ceremony. The bride served tea with sweetmeats and reverently bowed to members of her husband's family in the following order: his paternal grandfather and grandmother, his maternal grandfather and grandmother, his father and mother, his paternal uncles and aunts by rank, his brothers and sisters-in-law, his brothers-in-law and sisters, and finally, other relatives and friends in no particular order.

A sumptuous dinner was then served for the family and guests. The shy blushing bride did not participate in the feast and remained in her bedchamber. The groom's parents rejoiced and were congratulated, for they had acquired a daughter-in-law. Guests walked in and out of the bridal chamber and made complimentary remarks about her beauty, charm and grace or teased and played tricks on the bride 玩新娘.

On the third day following the marriage, the bride and groom paid a visit to her parents. They brought gifts including cakes and a whole roast pig. Some of the cakes and parts of the roast pig, the head and hind portion with trotters, were given back to the couple when they returned home.

Birthday Customs

The birth of a son was a happy event in a Chinese family. Sons, especially the first-born, were highly regarded as family assets. They insured the continuation of the family name and the worship of the ancestral spirits. Sons would remain in the family and help with the family work, guaranteeing that parents and grandparents would be cared for in old age. In many families, particularly the families of poor peasants, daughters were considered to be liabilities and were discriminated against while still in the cradle. Good morsels of food and toys would be provided for sons but not for daughters. A daughter impoverished the family because she was an additional mouth to feed and obligated her parents to provide her with a dowry when she married. After marriage, she left her family and became a member of another family.

Some parents regarded their daughters as nonentities. They were not given names but were simply listed numerically—the oldest girl 大妹, number two girl 二妹, number three girl

三妹 and so on. When a Chinese was asked about his family, he often mentioned only his sons and omitted any reference to his daughters.

A newborn infant son was not considered a member of society until he was one month old. A month after birth, he was given a name. His head was shaved either by an elder, a grandparent or his mother. The child, dressed in a red gown, was then carried to the temple by his father. In the temple, his father notified the gods and the spirits of his ancestors of the birth of a son. He also notified the local Earth God 土地 because this god served as a spiritual registrar keeping a record of births, marriages and deaths. Incense and candles would be presented at the altar, accompanied by paper offerings and foods. In addition, there were special offerings of steamed buns, hard-boiled chicken eggs tinted red, sliced sweet pickled ginger and sometimes a whole roast pig. After the ceremony was concluded, the roast pig and other foods were taken home. The roast pig was then chopped into gift-size pieces for distribution together with the other foods to relatives and friends who had given gifts to the baby. A festive dinner was often hosted in the evening by the parents and grandparents of the baby to celebrate the joyous event. Red-tinted hard-boiled eggs and sliced pickled ginger, symbols of a new birth, were served with the feast.

The next celebration for the child was held on the first anniversary of his birth. At this gathering of relatives and friends, red-tinted hard-boiled eggs and sliced pickled ginger were again served with dinner.

After celebrating the first anniversary of the child's birth, no special attention was given to subsequent birthdays. On those days, however, it was not uncommon for a small gift to be presented to the child by his parents and a few special dishes would be prepared for the family dinner.

When a boy reached the marriageable age of sixteen, subsequent birthdays became progressively more important. Adult males celebrated their "big birthdays" 大生日 at the beginning of each decade of life—twenty-one, thirty-one, fifty-one, sixty-one and so on. The forty-first birthday was ignored completely because the word for four, *szu* 四, and the word for death, *ssu* 死, were close homonyms. The odd number at the beginning of each decade was considered propitious for men because odd numbers represented yang 陽, the active or positive male principle. For this reason, some people maintained that women should celebrate their big birthdays at ages twenty, thirty, fifty, sixty and so on because even numbers represented yin 陰, the passive or negative female principle.

The big birthdays were to be celebrated on or before but not after the actual date of the birthday. The older the honoree, the more elaborate the celebration. With advancement into each decade of life, the person received more gifts and greater homage from family, relatives and friends. At age fifty-one, the prized gift for a man from his children was a large, multipaneled wooden screen decorated with the symbols of longevity. The carved symbols were inlaid with enamel, ivory, silver or mother-of-pearl. The honoree and his wife sat in front of the screen while he received congratulations and honors.

The sixty-first birthday was a very important event that was celebrated with great rejoicing. At age sixty-one, the individual was considered to have completed a full "sixty-year cycle" 花甲子. He was now starting his second cycle.

At this birthday, the prized gift from a man's children was a coffin, to be kept at home or at a nearby temple. This gift provided the honoree the assurance that no matter what happened to the family in the future, he would be properly buried. To be properly buried was extremely important to the Chinese.

When a man reached his seventy-first birthday, he was permitted to wear an official robe and a cap affixed with a copper button. He was also granted the privilege of using a walking cane with the carving of a pigeon or dove on a jade handle. The pigeon and dove were secondary symbols of longevity.

At age eighty-one, the district or village elder notified the emperor of this venerable man's birthday. The emperor then ordered a memorial arch 牌樓 to be built in his honor. The cost of the memorial arch was paid for by the imperial treasury. Those who were ninety-one years of age or older were honored with greetings sent four times a year by the district magistrate.

Birthdays were also celebrated after the individual's death. Ordinary posthumous birthdays were observed at the family altar by presenting incense, candles, paper offerings and food before the tablet of the deceased. On big birthdays, the rites were held at the ancestral altar and a small banquet usually followed in the evening. Some people believed that after the ninety-first birthday, it was no longer necessary to continue with the posthumous birthday ceremonies, for by then the soul of the dead person had left the earth.

The primary symbols of longevity were the character for longevity, *shou* 壽, which could be written and stylized in many different ways; the Star God of Longevity; the stag; the Manchurian crane; the peach; the pine tree and long noodles. The stag was a symbol of longevity because it was believed that its coat turned gray after a life span of one thousand years, and pure white after another five hundred years. After two thousand years, its horns turned black and the animal achieved immortality. The Manchurian crane, a white bird with long legs, a long neck and a black head tinged scarlet on the top, was thought to be immortal. This crane was often depicted carrying a magical peach of immortality 仙桃 in its beak. The peaches of immortality were believed to come from the garden of the Royal Mother of the West 西王母 in the Western Heaven. Her peach trees sprouted leaves every three thousand years, and it took another three thousand years for the trees to bear ripe fruit. Eating one of these peaches conferred immortality.

The pine tree represented physical and mental well-being in old age because this hardy tree did not shed its leaves in winter, but remained green and thrived throughout the four seasons. Its bark was thought to resemble human skin in old age. It was also believed that the sap of a pine tree turned into amber when

Double peach medallion with symbols of longevity

the tree was one thousand years old. Incidentally, pine trees were often planted near a grave to protect the corpse, for it was believed that Wang Hsiang 罔象, a mythical animal that fed on the brains of the dead, had a great aversion to pine trees.

The long noodles served at birthday dinners to symbolize longevity were called "long-life noodles" 長壽麵. These could be wheat noodles or rice vermicelli 粉絲, but in either case the long strands were not broken or cut during cooking and serving.

Funeral Customs

Public health statutes and the passage of time have changed the old Taoist customs connected with death, mourning, funerals and burial of the dead. These customs have been modified and in many cases discarded.

In old China, the Chinese hardwood coffin, which was indispensable for interring the dead, was made from a section of a large straight log. After death, the corpse was placed in the wooden coffin, which was sealed. It then remained in the home for forty-nine days until the day of the burial.

A white cotton sash, placed across the top of the main door, and two lanterns, one on each side of the door, warned visitors that a death had recently occurred in the family. Mourners wore sackcloth robes and straw slippers. Women, in addition, wore sackcloth hoods over their heads. Men tied white cotton sashes around their foreheads and around their waists.

Mourners sat on the floor alongside the coffin. Professional wailers were employed to cry aloud when visitors entered the hall to pay their respects to the dead and to express their condolences to the family. The wake lasted throughout the night. The long ceremonies were conducted by Taoist priests, accompanied by musicians playing eerie music.

The funeral cortege proceeded to the burial site in the following order: men bearing lanterns inscribed with the family name and the age of the deceased, gong beaters, musicians, men carrying red boards with the titles of the deceased and his ancestors written in gold characters, a portrait of the deceased carried in a sedan-chair and a wooden tablet with the name of the deceased in the following sedan-chair. Next came the eldest son walking ahead of the coffin, carrying in one hand a wooden staff if it was his father's funeral, or a bamboo staff if it was his mother's funeral. In his other hand, he carried a bamboo pole with a streamer summoning the animal soul 魄 to accompany the body to the grave. Then came the coffin, borne by porters, and followed by the sons, daughters-in-law, daughters, relatives and friends.

The corpse was often buried at a site that had been preselected by the deceased, possibly with the aid of a geomancer. The period of mourning lasted two years and seven months.

Graves were sometimes exhumed and the remains reinterred in another location if the previous grave site was deemed to be unfavorable. An unfavorable grave site could cause illness and misfortune within the family. Also, it sometimes happened that a family might wish to have the bones of the deceased, which had been buried elsewhere, disinterred and returned to the ancestral village.

Today the traditional Taoist rites and ceremonies associated with funerals have been considerably simplified. The following description is an account of funeral customs observed in Hawaii in recent years.

Generally, when death appeared to be imminent, the family gave the dying person a ceremonial bath. The warm bath water was mildly scented and purified with a few fragrant pomelo leaves. After the bath, the dying person was dressed in burial clothes 壽衣 so that the body entering the next world would be clean and fully clothed. Many of the elderly, especially women, prepared for death by selecting their burial garments in advance. These garments were carefully wrapped in plain muslin and stored in a trunk or in the recess of a closet.

Immediately after death, the lights on the front porch and in the main hall were turned on. All the pictures decorating the home were either turned front side back or covered with white paper. All red decorations in the home were removed.

The undertaker was called to transfer the body from the home to the mortuary. Before the undertaker removed the corpse from the home, he or a family member lit three incense sticks and a pair of candles and burned a paper offering in the courtyard. This was done to ward off evil spirits while en route to the mortuary.

All the members of the family were promptly notified of the death. Those living away from home were summoned. To express their grief and sorrow, mourners changed into somber clothes and women omitted cosmetics. Any kind of festivity, such as listening to music or good news, visiting with friends, going to the theater or attending social functions, was considered improper. In addition, the marriage of a son or daughter was prohibited throughout the mourning period.

The Chinese traditionally buried their dead in hardwood coffins. Metal caskets were not used. A full-couch coffin with a removable cap was selected for a traditional Chinese funeral. Visitors viewed the deceased by walking around the coffin. In a Christian funeral, by contrast, a hinged-panel coffin is used because the body is viewed from the right side.

A Taoist priest specializing in funerals was consulted for selection of an auspicious day for the funeral and burial. After casting a horoscope, he was able to determine when the spirit soul 魂 left the body of the dying, the form the soul would take in the next world, the evening when the departed soul returned home for a visit with the family 廻陽 and the numerical ages that would be in conflict with the deceased 相冲. This same priest also conducted the funeral ceremony.

The Chinese believed that the spirit soul usually left the body of the dying before the bodily functions ceased. This soul might then ascend to Heaven 打天道 or return to earth 打地道. When returned to earth, the soul might be reincarnated in human form or as an animal with intestines such as a dog or pig, or even as an insect such as a large moth. It was also believed that the soul of the dead returned home to visit with the family shortly after death. If the soul was happy and content in the next world, the visit took place approximately twelve to fourteen days after death. However, if the soul was unhappy, the return visit was earlier, about six to seven days after death. People whose ages were in conflict with the deceased, especially family members, had to turn away and not look at the closing of the coffin and at the lowering of the coffin into the grave. It was believed that the soul might recognize such individuals and hold them responsible for confining the body in the coffin and committing it to the ground. A vengeful spirit might then inflict illness and misfortune upon them.

On the day of the funeral, the ages that

would be in conflict with the deceased were posted outside the funeral hall. In the hall, at the middle of the far end opposite the main entrance, the coffin was placed on a bier with the cap removed. Cloth funeral scrolls 祭輓 received from relative and friends decorated the walls of the hall. The foot end of the coffin faced the entrance area where the visitors sat. Ample room was provided so that visitors could walk around the opened coffin while viewing the body.

The fully dressed corpse was placed straight in the coffin with arms and hands alongside the body. The body was often adorned with gold, jade and pearl jewelry. Rings and bracelets were commonly seen on older individuals of both sexes. Older women often wore a black head band 頭包 decorated with a pearl or a piece of jade, hairpins and earrings. Sometimes a pearl was placed between the lips of a woman, or a coin between the lips of a man. It was believed that jade and pearls protected the body from decay and provided light for the soul.

Layers of paper coverlets 壽被 with the character for longevity 壽 inscribed in bluish-green or gold ink were placed over the body. These paper coverlets were provided and paid for by the widow, daughters-in-law and daughters of the deceased.

Two lighted oil lamps were placed under the coffin. One was placed under the head 頭燈, and the other under the feet 脚燈. These lamps provided light for the soul.

On the floor, at the foot end of the coffin, an altar was set up and various offerings placed upon it. It was believed that the soul, in the next world, still had certain needs. Facing the coffin on the right were a paper model of a gold mountain 金山, a dish of sweetmeats and a paper model of a male servant with a towel draped over his arm. On the left side were a paper model of a silver mountain 銀山, a large bowl of cooked rice with a pair of chopsticks inserted vertically and a paper model of a maid holding a tray with two cups of tea. At the center, also on the floor, were a sandbox with incense and candles, a cup of tea, a cup of wine, a large dish containing a boiled chicken with its head and beak pointing toward the coffin and another dish containing a piece of boiled pork and two boiled duck eggs. A short distance from these offerings, on the left, was a large receptacle used for the burning of paper offerings, paper funerary money and paper representations of gold and silver ingots.

Before the beginning of the funeral ceremony, the family members assembled in the hall. Men dressed in dark clothing with black mourning bands 黑紗 pinned around their left arm. Women wore white and had black mourning bows pinned over their right breast.

The oldest son enacted the old ceremony of "purchasing water" 買水 from a brook owned by the Dragon King of the Sea 海龍王. Equipped with a small pan containing funerary money called "brook money" 溪錢, he led the family through the front door of the hall to the outside. There, three incense sticks and a pair of candles were lit and a paper offering burned. An attendant poured water over the brook money in the pan. The oldest son then led the family back into the hall and "washed the face" of the deceased with the moistened funerary money.

The family then assembled alongside the coffin with the men sitting to the left of the deceased and the women to the right. The oldest son sat nearest the head of the coffin and was followed by the other sons, sons-in-law and grandsons according to rank. On the opposite side, the widow sat nearest to the head of the coffin, followed by the daughters-in-law, daughters and granddaughters according to rank. The priest chanted and offered prayers to "open the road" 開路 for the departed soul.

Visitors who came to pay their last respects presented gifts of incense, paper offerings, cut flowers or money enclosed in a white envelope. Upon entering the hall, each visitor received a piece of candy and a red paper packet 封包 containing a five-cent coin. The candy was eaten to "sweeten" the sorrow and to counteract the bitterness of death. The red paper packet symbolized "good luck and happiness" and the five-cent coin had to be spent as soon as possible to buy something sweet. Visitors were escorted to the coffin where they paid their respects to the deceased by bowing reverently three times and then walked around the coffin counterclockwise, expressing their sympathy to the family and viewing the body.

The "presentation of rice" 贈飯 ceremony was performed to provide rice and liquor for the departed soul in the next world. For this ceremony, a table was set up at the foot end of the coffin, upon which were placed a sandbox with burning incense sticks, a plate of cooked rice with lotus seeds 蓮子 and red jujubes 紅棗, a cup of water, four cups of liquor and an empty crock. The priest took the bowl of cooked rice with the pair of chopsticks inserted vertically from its place on the floor and transferred the rice into the crock, adding liquor and water to it. Then each family member, according to seniority, added a bowl of cooked rice from the plate of rice containing the lotus seeds and red jujubes. After the rice was served by the family, more liquor was added and the crock was covered with a piece of white cloth and a piece of red cloth. The crock was then sealed.

Later it would be taken to the cemetery and buried with the coffin in the grave.

At the end of the service, all the visitors walked around the coffin for a final viewing. They were followed by the family. During the closing of the coffin, everyone turned away while the priest summoned the animal soul to accompany the body to the grave.

After the closing of the coffin, a long strip of red cloth 棺材紅 was draped longitudinally over it, and six pallbearers wearing white cotton gloves transported the coffin to the hearse. The family members, according to seniority, followed by relatives and friends accompanied the hearse on the procession to the cemetery. The attendant riding in the hearse scattered paper funerary money 放路錢 along the way in order to appease malevolent spirits and persuade them not to harm the deceased.

Traditionally, the most propitious site for a cemetery was the slope of a hill where the water drainage was good and the two sides were bounded by hills. Toward the lowland fronting the cemetery, the view ideally included a body of water such as a river, pond, lake or ocean. In a Chinese cemetery, married couples were usually buried side by side and the burial sites occupied the back, center and front areas. Unmarried adults, children and infants were buried in specially designated areas adjacent to the left and right boundaries of the cemetery.

At the cemetery, the six pallbearers removed the coffin from the hearse and placed it over the open grave with the foot end pointing toward the lowland. It was believed that the corpse would repose comfortably in this position. Fronting the foot of the grave and on the ground was a temporary altar with burning incense and candles and a low stand with food offerings. This stand was set with five cups of tea, five cups of wine, five bowls of rice, five pairs of chopsticks and five dishes of food. The five dishes of food were usually fish, chicken, *tou fu*, prawns and pot roast pork 扣肉.

The priest and family assembled in front of the altar while friends gathered around the grave. The priest chanted and made offerings. He prayed and summoned the soul to accompany the body into the grave. The coffin was then slowly lowered into the grave. Again, the family and friends would turn away during the lowering of the coffin into the grave. After the coffin was lowered, the funeral director checked to verify that it was properly aligned. The sealed crock containing the cooked rice and liquor was placed in a niche dug at the foot of the grave, and grains of uncooked rice were tossed into the grave by the priest and family members. The pallbearers threw in their white cotton gloves. Finally, the priest concluded the burial ceremony by urging the family to follow the example set by the life of the deceased. As people left the cemetery, they were each given a piece of candy and a five-cent coin wrapped in red paper.

If the deceased was elderly, family and friends were often invited to a lunch, usually held in a restaurant, following the burial. After lunch, everyone took home some leftover food in his used rice bowl and chopsticks. To carry the food, each guest was provided with a paper sack containing two oranges and a ten-cent coin wrapped in red paper. This custom derives from the time when people traveled long distances on foot to attend the funeral and burial services. The leftover food and oranges would serve as nourishment and the coin was used to buy something sweet during the long journey home. When people who had been to a funeral arrived at home, they purified them-

selves before entering the house by washing their face and eyes with water purified with pomelo leaves and stepping over a small fire fueled with paper, straw or dried leaves.

Many families held a ceremony when the departed spirit soul returned to his home for a visit with the family. This ceremony was held in the evening of the day designated by the priest. The windows and doors were opened. Lights on the porch and in the halls were turned on to welcome the soul. At the family altar, incense sticks and candles were lit and paper offerings burned. The soul's arrival was indicated by certain signs: the window curtains might stir with the breeze, the candles might flicker, or an insect, especially a large moth, might fly in, attracted by the light. The ceremony usually lasted several hours and ended when the incense sticks and candles were completely burned.

The duration of the mourning period varied, depending on the wishes of the family. Some families held the ceremony to end the period of mourning 脫孝 immediately after the burial. Others held it three days or one month after the burial.

If the mourning period was to end immediately after the burial, the deceased was notified of this at the altar beside the grave. Three incense sticks and a pair of candles were lit. These and a pair of gold tinsel flowers with red pistils 花紅 were set in the ground a short distance from the foot of the grave. A dish of sweetmeats was set on the ground and paper offerings were burned. This was done to appease hungry ghosts and to protect the soul in the fresh grave from them. Then the family faced the hill and bowed three times before removing and burning the black mourning bands and bows. To light the way home, every married son was presented with a flashlight and every daughter-in-law with a flashlight and a comb. The comb, *shu* 梳, alluded to *po so* 婆娑, meaning the descendants will branch off like a tree and prosper. Every member of the family was given a sprig of aromatic juniper 扁栢 tied with a red ribbon. Women either pinned it on their dress or used it to adorn the hair. The men usually placed it in a pocket. The short ceremony was concluded with the burning of a packet of firecrackers. On leaving, everyone was given a twenty-five-cent coin wrapped in red paper.

The ceremony to end the mourning period three days after the burial was held in the cemetery with the altar and the same food offerings at the grave, and was identical to that described for the end of mourning immediately after buri-al. The ceremony to end mourning one month after burial was held in the home at the family altar. Incense, candles, paper offerings, food offerings and rites were the same as those described above except that the offerings to the hungry ghosts were omitted.

If the end of the mourning period was one month after the burial, some families celebrated with a feast. Family members, relatives, and close friends were all invited to attend the dinner. This was a happy occasion. Women wore red or colorful clothes, styled their hair and resumed the use of cosmetics and jewelry. After all, everything had been done for the loved one who had passed away. All the proper rites and ceremonies had been performed. The deceased was now at peace. The future belonged to the living.

CHAPTER 10

Chinese Hells

The Chinese originally had little conception of the fate of the soul after death. They believed that it just roamed aimlessly on earth. New ideas of judgment, punishment, hell, reincarnation and the attainment of a state of absolute blessedness called nirvana were all introduced by Buddhist missionaries from India in the first century A.D.

Subsequently, the Chinese invented their own hells or earth prisons 地獄. Like the Hindu and Buddhist hells, these hells were temporary prisons where the souls of sinners who had violated moral laws were judged, sentenced and punished. After a certain period of time, which varied according to the offense, every soul imprisoned in hell had to leave and be reincarnated. In contrast, the Christian and Islamic hells were places of eternal punishment where sinners had no hope for redemption, release or salvation. Thus, to some degree, Chinese hells were similar to the Purgatory of the Roman Catholic faith in that Purgatory was a temporary state. Individuals who died in the grace of God but without having fully made amends for their failings had to atone for their sins by suffering in Purgatory prior to their admission to heaven. Like the Chinese, Catholics believed that these sufferings could be ameliorated by prayer.

At first, the Buddhists had only eight hells. These hells were situated at the foot of a mountain near the edge of the universe. Each hell measured approximately 5,000 to 8,000 feet on each side. Later, the number of hells gradually increased. Some claimed that there were a total of over 84,000 hells, of which 128 were hot, 8 were cold, 8 were dark and the rest were miscellaneous. There were many different accounts of these Chinese hells.

During the Sung 宋 dynasty (960–1279), a Taoist scholar made the hells distinctively Chinese by relocating them from near the edge of the universe to a place under a high mountain near the city of Feng Tu 酆都 in Szechuan 四川 province in southwest China. In this new conception, the Taoist-Buddhist hells were divided into ten kingdoms or courts. Each was ruled by a king who sat on a throne surrounded by ministers and attendants. Each king judged specific types of offenses and meted out punishments accordingly.

During the reign of Emperor Wan Li 萬曆 (1573–1620) of the Ming 明 dynasty, a governor of Szechuan named Kuo 郭 forced open the entrance to hell and found a deep vertical shaft. It was said that he then fashioned a box, sat in it, and with the aid of a rope, descended into the passage. After lowering himself about two hundred feet, he reached the bottom of the shaft and found the ground covered with rich vegetation. The view was spectacular. Exploring the area, he found an iron gate which led to the first court. He knocked on the gate and was greeted by Kuan Ti 關帝, the God of War.

Kuan Ti escorted Governor Kuo and gave him a detailed visit through the first five courts. At the fifth court, he met Yen-Lo Wang 閻羅王, who told him that souls, regardless of position and rank, had to be punished for sins committed on earth. After the visit through the first five courts, Kuan Ti bade him goodbye. The governor returned to the box, hoisted himself up through the shaft and returned to the surface of the earth. He then recorded everything he had seen in hell.

The first court was ruled by Chin-Kwang Wang 秦廣王, whose birthday was on the first day of the second moon. Deeds of the lost souls recorded in the Register of Life and Death 生死簿 were reviewed in this court, which was a kind of antechamber to the other courts. Virtuous souls and those with a few minor sins who had repented and made amends bypassed the other courts and were sent directly to the tenth court for release and reincarnation. Evil souls were made to view their past misdeeds in a large mirror suspended in midheaven.

The second court, the Great Cold Hell, was presided over by Chu-Chiang Wang 楚江王, whose birthday was on the first day of the third moon. He judged cases involving priests who lured children from their homes to make them monks, husbands who abandoned their wives under false pretenses, people who illegally disposed of property entrusted to their care, charlatans acting as physicians, officials who oppressed people and those who used weapons carelessly and injured people. As punishment, the guilty were thrown into a cold, icy pond.

The third court, the Hell of Black Ropes, was headed by Sung-Ti Wang 宋帝王, whose birthday was on the eighth day of the second moon. His jurisdiction involved ministers who were ungrateful to their emperor, wives who were ungrateful to their husbands, disobedient and unworthy sons and rebellious soldiers. He also had jurisdiction over disobedient slaves, geomancers who gave false opinions regarding sites selected for houses and graves, farmers who desecrated graves by plowing over them and turning up coffins, people who refused to worship their ancestors, forgers and perjurers. Those guilty of such crimes were fed to tigers, pierced with arrows or disemboweled.

The fourth court was ruled by Wu-Kuan Wang 五官王. He was honored on the eighteenth day of the second moon. People who did not pay their rent or taxes, physicians who prescribed inferior medicines, those who willfully or maliciously destroyed crops, priests who violated their vows, prostitutes, gamblers, cheaters, counterfeiters and troublemakers were tried in this court. The guilty were thrown into a large lake of blood, pounded in a mortar or suspended from a beam by hooks which were passed through their flesh.

The ruler of the fifth court was the renowned and stern Yen-Lo Wang 閻羅王. His birthday was on the eighth day of the first moon. Adopted by the Buddhists, he was originally the old Hindu god Yama, the Vedic God of the Dead. Before his deification, Yama had been the ruler of Vaisali, a kingdom in northern India. In a war with a neighboring country, and on the verge of defeat, Yama and his troops vowed that if the spirits of hell helped them defeat the enemy, they would be willing to be reborn in hell. Yama and his soldiers were victorious. Although Yama was deified as the Ruler of Hell, he and his men still had to be punished for their past crimes. Hot molten copper was poured down their throats every eight hours.

Actually, Yen-Lo Wang was originally assigned to the first court but was transferred to the fifth court because of his leniency in allowing souls to bypass the courts and go directly to the tenth court for release and reincarnation. The fifth court judged cases involving disbelievers of the Buddhist doctrines, slanderers, arsonists and those who used abrasive language. Those found guilty were sawed to pieces.

The sixth court was presided over by Pien-Cheng Wang 卞城王, whose birthday was on the eighth day of the third moon. Cases tried in this court involved people who stole gold by scraping it off idols, people who did not respect the teachings of Confucius, those who deposited rubbish and filth in the vicinity of temples, readers of pornographic literature, those who wasted rice and those who blasphemed Heaven, Earth and the North Star. The guilty were hung by the feet and had their skin stripped off, were sawed into pieces or were forced to kneel with uncovered knees on sharp spikes.

The seventh court was headed by Tai-Shan Wang 泰山王. His birthday was on the twenty-seventh day of the third moon. Old men who sucked the breasts of women, physicians who made medicines from human bones, grave robbers, oppressors of the poor and masters who mistreated their slaves were judged in this court. Punishment for the guilty included

throwing them into volcanos, boiling them in oil or placing a heavy wooden yoke around their necks and hands.

The ruler of the eighth court, the Great Hot Hell, was Tu-Ti Wang 都帝王. His birthday was observed on the seventh day of the first moon. Cases in this court involved people who neglected their parents, men who were ungrateful to their benefactors, those who engaged in obscene conversations and women who hung their clothes to dry on rooftops, thus interfering with the flight of spirits through the air. The guilty were trampled under the hooves of horses, were cut into pieces, had their tongues removed or were plunged into a lake of blood.

The ninth court was administered by Ping-Teng Wang 平等王, whose birthday was on the eighth day of the fourth moon. Artists who painted lewd pictures, priests who misused funds, people who sowed discord between husbands and wives, those who created dissension between parents and children and those who gave aphrodisiacs to women were tried in this court. The guilty were hurled onto sharp spikes, speared with a trident, gored by pigs or fed to wild animals.

The tenth court was under Chuan-Lun Wang 轉輪王, whose birthday was on the seventeenth day of the seventh moon. This last court was not for judgment and punishment. Instead, it was a chamber where souls were prepared for reincarnation. The idea of reincarnation was that a soul could be reborn as a being with intestines such as a human, an animal, fish or insect. Souls could also become gods, demons living underground or hungry ghosts wandering the earth. Souls were not reborn as trees, plants, stones or inanimate objects. The role of Chuan-Lun Wang was to determine the form of transmigration. Before release from hell, the soul was required to visit the kitchen of Grandmother Meng 孟婆. Here the soul drank a broth that caused it to forget all previous existences and experiences. Those that refused to drink the broth were force-fed by two strong attendants.

In the Sung dynasty, a Taoist priest wrote an imaginative account, *Yu Li Chao Chuan* 玉歷鈔傳, which described in detail another version of the soul's journey through hell. This journey was divided into seven periods of seven days each, or a total of forty-nine days.

During the first week, a soul was led to Demon Barrier Pass 鬼門關. At the pass, the devils commanding the barrier demanded money. If the money offered was adequate, the soul was allowed to proceed. If inadequate, the soul was stripped and beaten.

In the second week, the soul reached a bridge where it was weighed. The good and virtuous were weightless and escaped punishment. The bad and wicked weighed heavily and were sawed to pieces or ground into powder.

In the third week, the soul arrived at Bad Dog Village 惡狗村. A good soul was greeted and welcomed by friendly dogs wagging their tails. An evil soul was met by fierce angry dogs snarling and tearing it to pieces until the blood flowed like a river.

During the fourth week, the soul was brought before the large Mirror of Retribution 業鏡. This mirror revealed the future. The good soul saw innocence and beauty. The bad soul saw its reincarnation as a loathsome animal, such as a pig wallowing in mud or a snake slithering through the grass.

By the fifth week, the soul begged to be allowed to return to life as a human being but was told by the escorting god that it was no longer fit to mingle with uncorrupted mortals. The soul was now allowed a glimpse of its former family's activities. This was a painful experience because the soul realized that it had lost its place within the family.

During the sixth week, the soul arrived at the Bridges of the Inevitable River 奈河橋. These bridges spanned a chasm which was 100,000 feet deep. At the bottom was a river with whirlpools and rapids. Large snakes raised their heads high out of the water as they searched for human flesh. A good soul was escorted across the chasm by way of a gold and silver bridge. The wicked soul was forced, by attendants using clubs, to cross the chasm by straddling a thin rope about 1.3 inches in diameter.

In the seventh week, the soul was brought to the court of Chuan-Lun Wang, where it petitioned for reincarnation, drank the broth prepared by Grandmother Meng and finally was released from hell.

Stories describing the frightful punishments administered in hell were often told to children to encourage them to lead virtuous lives. In addition, scrolls depicting the judgments and punishments of hell were often hung on the wall during traditional Taoist funeral services. Incense, paper spirit money, paper representations of gold and silver ingots and prayers were offered to the rulers of hell and the souls of the dead. It was believed that these offerings could bring about leniency from judges and lighter sentences for the souls of the departed.

CHAPTER 11

Discoveries and Inventions

During the ancient and medieval ages, China had a highly advanced civilization. The Chinese made significant discoveries in the fields of astronomy, meteorology, physics, chemistry, the natural and biological sciences, medicine and engineering. Many of these discoveries trickled slowly into Europe by way of the Silk Road and the Middle East. From the Middle East, they reached Europe by two routes. One route was north of the Mediterranean Sea through the Balkans; the other was south of the Mediterranean through North Africa and then across the sea to Europe.

It is generally agreed that the Chinese were the first to invent the magnetic compass, paper, gunpowder and printing. These major inventions, as well as some of the less well known but interesting Chinese discoveries, are discussed below in chronological order.

The Magnetic Compass

Some Chinese have claimed that the Duke of Chou 周公 discovered the magnetic compass in 1110 B.C. when he invented the "south-pointing chariot" 指南車, a vehicle supporting a figure

of a man with an outstretched arm. Regardless of the direction of the chariot, the arm always pointed south. It was said that this chariot helped the tribute-bearing envoys from Tongking in Southeast Asia find their way back home from China. The claim that the chariot was a magnetic compass is not correct. Most authorities believe that the chariot was actually a mechanical device using a system of differential gears to maintain a direction once it had been set. The south-pointing chariot was a remarkable invention but not a magnetic compass.

About one thousand years later, in the first or second century B.C., the Chinese were experimenting with the magnetic properties of magnetite or lodestone 攝石, a hard black rock. Geomancers made a "south-pointing spoon" from this stone and used it for divination. When placed on a smooth bronze plate, the spoon invariably rotated to a north-south axis. Later it was discovered that if a long piece of lodestone was pierced through a small piece of wood and floated on water, the piece of lodestone assumed a north-south axis; the same thing would happen if a long piece of lodestone was balanced on an upright pin. It was further

South-pointing lodestone spoon

discovered that the magnetic properties of lodestone could be transferred to a small piece of iron by placing the stone close to it or, better still, when they touched each other.

It was just another step to the discovery that an iron needle could be magnetized by heating it and then cooling it in the north-south axis. A magnetic needle was used to make the first magnetic compass, called the "south-pointing needle" 指南針, for purposes of geomancy. Then, sometime in the tenth century A.D., the Chinese used the "south-pointing needle" for navigation. The first mention of the magnetic compass in Europe was in 1190.

Paper

Despite the fact that the word paper is derived from papyrus, the name of the water plant used by the ancient Egyptians to make a material for writing, paper was first produced in China. Historians have agreed that this event occurred in A.D. 105 when Tsai-Lun 蔡倫, the chief eunuch under Emperor Ho Ti 和帝, boiled a mixture of fragmented mulberry tree bark, hemp trimmings, old linens and old fish nets to make a pulp which was then pounded into a paste and dried in sheets to form crude paper.

Gradually the quality of this crude paper was improved. Through leaching, polishing and glazing, Chinese paper became smooth, soft, fine and strong. The Europeans who first saw this improved paper thought it was made from silk.

Before the development of paper, the Chinese wrote on bamboo tablets, wooden slabs and silk cloths. With paper they had a cheaper and better material to write on. During the Tang 唐 dynasty (618–906), the use of paper was widespread.

The knowledge of how to make paper slowly spread westward and eventually reached Europe. Paper appeared in Central Asia in the third century. In 751 the Chinese fought the Moors in Samarkand. The Chinese lost the battle and many were captured. These Chinese prisoners taught the Moors the art of making paper.

Papermaking spread to Egypt around the year 900. In 1150, about one thousand years after the invention of paper in China, papermaking spread northward from Egypt across the Mediterranean Sea to Europe.

Many people have considered paper to be the most significant Chinese contribution to world civilization. The relative cheapness of paper made it possible for books to be printed and made available to the masses. Now, of course, there are countless products made of paper.

Gunpowder

Gunpowder 火藥, the oldest explosive, was probably developed by Chinese alchemists in the sixth century. This black powder was made from a compound of potassium nitrate, charcoal and sulfur. When ignited it burned rapidly and produced a cloud of smoke.

Gunpowder was first used to make firecrackers for religious ceremonies. Later, the Chinese may have used it to make crude bombs and grenades. By the twelfth century, gunpowder was used to launch the fiery rockets called "fire arrows" 火箭. In the thirteenth and fourteenth centuries, the Mongols may have used the explosive to propel projectiles from guns and cannons.

The exact steps for making gunpowder were unknown to the West until Friar Roger Bacon wrote a book in 1242 detailing them. In 1300 gunpowder was used in guns and cannons, and it remained the only military explosive for over five hundred years. In 1600 it was used for industrial blasting.

Modern gunpowder is usually made with 75 percent potassium nitrate, 15 percent charcoal and 10 percent sulfur. When used as a blasting powder, which requires a less powerful explosion, the percentage of potassium nitrate is reduced. Since the mid-1800s, many new explosive compounds have been developed, such as dynamite, smokeless powder, TNT (trinitrotoluene) and other highly complex compounds. These have replaced gunpowder for military and industrial uses. Gunpowder, however, is still used to make firecrackers, fireworks, time fuses to ignite smokeless powder and powder for ceremonial cannon salutes.

Printing

Around the year 750, six centuries after the invention of paper, block printing with ink on paper was invented in West China. The earliest extant printed text is a Buddhist sutra produced in 868.

Around the middle of the eleventh century, the Chinese invented a form of printing with movable type but this method of printing did not develop further. Block printing, the preferred method, was better suited for Chinese characters. In block printing, the characters needed for an entire page were carved on a slab of wood or earthenware and then inked for printing.

Ink was made in China as early as 1000 B.C. The soot-and-resin ink used in writing and printing was formed into sticks or tablets. The solid ink was then converted into a liquid by grinding it in water. The early Chinese ink was of poor quality. In A.D. 620, the king of Korea presented to the emperor of China several pieces of high-quality ink made from lampblack that had been collected from burnt-down old pine and mixed with stag-horn glue. The Chinese tried to make this type of ink for themselves but were not successful until about three centuries later.

Like paper, printing reached the West slowly. It reached Europe in 1375, just before the time of Gutenberg. Johann Gutenberg (1400–1468) was born in Mainz, Germany. He was from a noble family and is credited with the invention of printing with movable type. Prior to that, all printing in Europe was done through block printing. The success of Gutenberg's invention may be due in large part to the fact that Western alphabets are particularly suited to this type of printing. It is interesting to note that the Constance Missal, dating from around 1450, is now thought to be the earliest European book printed with movable type, preceding the Gutenberg Bible by several years.

Silk

A very interesting specialty of the Chinese was insect culture. Insects were raised for many purposes. From ancient times, bees were raised for their wax, from which candles were made, and for their honey, used in medicines. The scale insect, *Ericus sinesis*, was bred for its scales of white wax, which were also used for making candles and medicines. The scale lac and insects similar to the cochneal bug were raised for making dyes. Crickets were kept and cultivated for the sport of cricket fighting.

The most important insect culture by far, however, was the breeding of silkworms for silk production. The origin of sericulture—the raising of silkworms and the production of silk—lies shrouded in the mist of prehistory. According to legend, Lady Hsi-Ling 西陵氏, the consort of Huang Ti 黄帝, the Yellow Emperor (2698–2598 B.C.), noticed in her garden a fat worm on a mulberry tree swaying its head back and forth, spitting out a delicate fiber. The fiber formed a cocoon and encased the worm. She picked up the cocoon, dropped it into her cup of hot tea and discovered that she was able to unwind a continuous fiber from the softened cocoon. Looking at the delicate fiber, she wondered how she would look clothed in a gown made from such fiber. She decided to ask the emperor for a grove of mulberry trees so that she could raise the worms and produce thousands of cocoons. After experimenting, she was able to produce enough fiber to weave a piece of silk cloth, which she made into a beautiful gown.

Strictly speaking, the silkworm is not a worm but a caterpillar, the larva of a moth. All caterpillars produce silk fibers but they vary considerably in quality. The best silk fiber comes from the caterpillar of the *Bombyx mori*, a rather large white moth with black-lined wings that measure about two inches from wing tip to wing tip. This caterpillar only eats white mulberry leaves. Each spring when the leaves appear on the white mulberry tree, the eggs of the *Bombyx mori* are taken out of cold storage and incubated. After about ten days of incubation, the eggs hatch into tiny hairlike larvae about one-eighth to one-quarter of an inch in length. The larvae are fed fresh white mulberry leaves which they eat continuously throughout the day and night, consuming their own weight in leaves daily. They grow rapidly and shed their skins four times. After about thirty-five days, a full-grown silkworm has increased its weight by about ten thousand times and measures two to three inches in length and one-half inch in thickness. At this stage, the caterpillar suddenly stops eating as it sways its head back and forth looking for a twig from which to spin its cocoon.

To spin the cocoon, two glands eject a viscous fluid through an opening located in the upper lip of the silkworm. When the sticky fluid comes into contact with the air it hardens into a fiber. This fiber is covered with a gummy substance called sericin. At the beginning, the silkworm spins the outer covering, the floss of the cocoon. It continues to wind the silk fiber around and around its body. As the silkworm spins, its body gradually decreases in size. After about five days of spinning, the cocoon is completed. In the process, the caterpillar changes into a pupa or the preadult stage of a moth. The pupa is completely enveloped in the cocoon.

Soon after the cocoons are completed, the best are selected for breeding. The remaining cocoons, used for silk production, are placed in a hot oven or a steam bath to kill the pupae and to prevent damage to the silk fibers of the cocoons. For silk production, about 50 percent of the cocoons are fine enough to produce delicate white-reeled silk. The remaining 50 percent are used to make "refuse silk," or silk of an inferior quality.

If the cocoon is not subjected to heat, the pupa develops into an adult moths in two to three weeks. The adult moth then ejects an enzyme that weakens the cocoon sufficiently for it to be able to break through the fibers and emerge from the cocoon.

Soon after the adult moths emerge, they mate. Several hours after mating, a female moth lays about three hundred to five hundred eggs the size of a pin-head on strips of special egg-laying paper. Once the eggs are laid, the moth dies within two to three days. The eggs are collected and kept in cold storage.

Cocoons used for silk production are graded and soaked in warm water to dissolve the sericin that holds the fibers together. Then the fibers are unwound. This is done by stirring the cocoons floating on the warm water with a bamboo comb to catch the loose ends of the fibers. Several fibers are collected to form a strand. This strand is then unwound from the cocoons and reeled. After reeling, the silk strands are twisted into skeins. The skeins are shipped to the factory where the raw silk is processed into fabrics.

In some cocoons, a silk fiber may be one thousand feet in length, but only about seven hundred feet of the silk fiber can be reeled. The fiber from the floss of the cocoon and the end of the cocoon must be spun. This spun silk is not as strong or shiny as reeled silk. Spun silk is generally used to manufacture rough silk fabrics, which are made into dress trimmings, hat bands, curtains and upholsteries. Interest-

ingly, about one thousand miles of silk fiber are required to make a pound of silk.

There are more than five hundred species of silkworms flourishing in the wild. They feed on a variety of foliage such as oak and castor-oil plant leaves. Moths from the wild silkworms are usually larger, prettier and more robust than the *Bombyx mori*. Some species grow up to six inches in length and the caterpillars spin egg-sized cocoons. Depending on the variety of the moth, the wild silkworm eggs hatch in anywhere from six weeks to twelve months, producing one to eight generations of silkworms a year. Generally, silk from wild silkworms is rough, not easily bleached or dyed, and cannot be reeled. The off-white silk from wild silkworms is called Tussah silk. Examples of Tussah silk are Silk Pongee and Silk Shantung.

Silk fiber is one of the strongest natural fibers. A silk thread is about two-thirds as strong as an iron wire of equal size. Silk is very flexible and extremely smooth; dirt cannot cling to it. The protein silk fiber is triangular in shape and it reflects light, giving silk fabrics a beautiful sheen.

Trade between China and Europe has continued since the second century B.C. The famous Silk Road leading through barren deserts and across treacherous mountain passes was so named because the main item of trade from China was always silk. As the "queen of textiles," silk was an expensive luxury item sought by emperors and aristocrats of ancient and medieval Europe. During the time of Julius Caesar in the first century B.C., silk was worth its weight in gold. Even today, the price of silk is almost twenty-five times the price of cotton. Because of its great commercial value, the secrets of sericulture were carefully guarded by the Chinese for many centuries. Death by torture was imposed by imperial decree on anyone who divulged the secrets to foreigners. Nevertheless, silkworms probably reached Japan by way of Korea early in the fourth century A.D.

According to one legend, the Byzantine emperor Justinian, in the sixth century, ordered several monks visiting China to bring back some silkworm eggs. The monks succeeded in carrying the eggs all the way to Constantinople by concealing them in hollow bamboo walking canes. These eggs, smuggled out of China, supposedly mark the beginning of silk production in the West. By the thirteenth century, the Italian cities of Lucca, Venice, Florence and Genoa had become silk centers. In the sixteenth century, France started silk production in the city of Lyon. In the eighteenth century, French Huguenots in London helped England produce silk.

Now, thirty-five countries produce silk, amounting to some 480,000 tons of cocoons annually. However, only 52,000 tons of silk are produced each year, a mere 0.2 percent of the world's annual textile fiber production. China leads the world in silk production, accounting for 36,000 tons of silk annually. China also produces about 80 percent of the world's Tussah silk. The other major silk-producing countries, in the order of productivity, are Japan, India, the U.S.S.R. and Korea.

Deep Borehole Drilling

In the landlocked province of Szechuan 四川, some 1,200 miles from the sea, the ancient Chinese could not depend on salt from the sea. As early as the second century B.C., they tapped the large brine deposits found deep under the earth's surface by drilling boreholes. As the method for drilling boreholes gradually im-

proved, they were also successful in drawing up natural gas which could be used for fuel.

By the eleventh century, the Chinese were able to drill boreholes exceeding three thousand feet in depth. The Chinese method of deep drilling was accomplished by a team of men jumping on and off a beam to impact the drilling bit while the boring tool was rotated by buffalo and oxen. The drilling was tedious and time consuming. Depending on the depth, the drilling of a single well might take as long as ten years.

The same method, called "Kicking Her Down," was used to drill the first petroleum well in California in the 1860s. According to one authority, Joseph Needham, the Chinese who were brought to California to help build the railroads at the beginning of the nineteenth century may have introduced this method of deep drilling to the Californians.

The Stern-post Rudder

Ancient water craft were primarily navigated through the use of oars held at an angle in the water, usually at the rear of the vessel. To steer their vessels more effectively, the Chinese invented the stern-post rudder 船舵. This rudder, fixed at the center of the stern, pivoted on an axis and could be turned in either direction to steer the vessel.

On the evidence of references contained in writings dating from the fifth and sixth centuries, it used to be assumed that the first stern-post rudder was invented sometime in the fifth century. But in 1958, the Academia Sinica and the Kwangtung 廣東 Provincial Museum jointly excavated several Late Han 後漢 tombs in the city of Canton 廣州. These tombs, dating from the first and second centuries A.D., contained many clay funerary figures, including an assemblage of beautiful pottery depicting in great detail the central axial stern-post rudder. Since earlier funerary ship models from the Chou 周 dynasty and the Early Han 前漢 all show the use of steering oars, it seems safe to conclude that the stern-post rudder was invented in the first century A.D.

In Europe the stern-post rudder did not come into use until the end of the twelfth century. By then the Chinese had improved the rudder in several ways. In the eleventh century, the balanced rudder made its appearance. This rudder had part of the vane in front of the axial post and part of it in back, making it easier for the helmsman to guide the vessel. This modification did not occur to the Europeans until the end of the eighteenth century.

Following the balanced rudder, the Chinese designed the fenestrated rudder. This was a rudder with windowlike openings of different shapes and sizes, the most common being a diamond-shaped fenestration. This rudder was easier to steer, reduced turbulence drag, did not affect efficiency and was hydrodynamically sound. The fenestrated rudder was not adopted in the West until the nineteenth century, when ships of iron and steel came into wide use.

The Seismograph

The seismograph 地震機 was invented in A.D. 132 to detect the tremors caused by earthquakes. The inventor, Chang Heng 張衡, was a learned scholar, a gifted artist and a poet, mathematician, geographer and astronomer.

His seismograph was a large domed bronze urn almost seven feet in diameter. On the exterior, around the urn and near the top, were eight bronze dragons, each with a movable

The first seismograph

lower jaw holding a small bronze ball. Directly below each dragon's mouth was a bronze toad looking upward with an open mouth. The interior of the urn contained the mechanism of the seismograph—essentially a series of heavy pendulums and levers.

When the instrument was activated by earthquake tremors, the pendulums swung and moved the levers. This reaction caused the release of one bronze ball from a dragon's mouth, which landed in the mouth of the toad, antomatically locking the mechanism against further action.

It was said that this seismograph was so sensitive that it could register earthquakes that otherwise went unnoticed. It could detect an earthquake in a distant area several days before couriers arrived at the capital with the news. The seismograph also indicated when and from what direction the earthquake tremors took place.

Chang Heng's seismograph preceded the first European seismograph by about 1,600 years.

The Horse Harness

A horse must be outfitted with a harness 馬具 before it can be used to pull a wagon or a load. For about five thousand years, from the time of the Sumerians in 4000 B.C. to the middle of the medieval period, draft horses in the West used the "throat and girth" harness. This type of harness exerted pressure on the throat of the animal, partially suffocating it and greatly reducing its pulling power.

In China, bas-reliefs from the Han 漢 dynasty (206 B.C.–A.D. 220) show the use of "breast-strap" harnesses on draft horses. The breast-strap harness is so named because the front of the harness was placed over the shoulder of the horse without exerting pressure on the throat. In the fifth century, the breast-strap harness was modified to such a degree that it received a new name, the "collar" harness. Compared to the throat and girth harness, the collar harness was far more efficient, doubling or even trebling the pulling power of the horse. By the thirteenth century, the modern collar harness was universally adopted in Europe.

The Wheelbarrow

Some authorities believe that the wheelbarrow 單輪手車 was invented by the warrior and statesman Chu-Ko Liang 諸葛亮 in A.D. 232. Others believe that it was invented earlier, perhaps in the first century B.C.

The simple and undistinguished wheelbarrow was an important labor-saving device. The single wheel of this vehicle substituted for a second individual when transporting small loads. In the Chinese wheelbarrow the load is carried on a flat rectangular wooden platform with the wheel located at the center of the cart.

A Chinese farm wheelbarrow

This type of wheelbarrow was used not only to transport freight but also to carry people who sat on it. With the wheel at the center, less effort was required to lift the load. In areas of China where the winds were favorable, a sail was attached to the barrow to help propel it.

The European wheelbarrow did not appear until about ten centuries later. This wheelbarrow was a triangular tublike receptacle with the wheel placed at the front. It was useful for transporting loads but not people. With the wheel at the front of the cart, greater effort was required to lift and push the load.

Iron-chain Suspension Bridge

The building of suspension bridges over rivers and gorges was not unique to China. People in South America built suspension bridges with liana, a long tough vine. People in western China and Tibet used twisted bamboo cables to build suspension bridges extending up to three hundred feet. The bamboo cables in these bridges had to be replaced about every fifty years.

The first iron-chain suspension bridge was built by the Chinese. Traditionally, the claim was made that a wrought iron-chain suspension bridge was constructed in the province of

Yunnan 雲南 in A.D. 65 and subsequently repaired in 1410. This claim cannot be substantiated. However, researchers have found proof that the first authentic iron-chain suspension bridge was built in Yunnan around the year 600. Documents relating to this bridge even contain the names of those who built it.

In Europe, iron-chain suspension bridges became fairly common after 1730. Fisher von Erlach of Leipzig, Germany, in 1725, had marveled at the Chinese iron-chain suspension bridge supposedly built in A.D. 65. A picture of this bridge was included in his book on architecture.

Porcelain

The evolution from crude pottery to porcelain 瓷器 took many thousands of years. Prehistoric and primitive societies made crude vessels and objects from clay. When moistened, molded and subjected to heat, clay contracts and hardens—a process that permanently changes its characteristics. The fired clay does not change to mud when it comes into contact with water, nor does it crumble when dried.

The earliest Chinese pottery that has been discovered so far is the neolithic painted pottery of the Yangshao 仰韶 culture, dating from 6000 B.C. In the evolution of Chinese pottery since then, three general types have emerged: earthenware, stoneware and porcelain.

Earthenware was the earliest type. It was made from unrefined, coarse clay and fired at a relatively low temperature, ranging from 800 to 1,000 degrees centigrade. Unglazed earthenware is thick, brittle and porous. When glazed, earthenware acquires a hard surface and becomes impervious to liquids.

Stoneware was a more advanced type of pottery. A fusible rock material containing feldspar and quartz was added to partially refined clay. Stoneware was fired at higher temperatures, ranging from 1,100 to 1,250 degrees centigrade. After firing, it was nonporous, stronger, harder and opaque; it frequently had a glasslike appearance.

Porcelain, for which China is famous, is a hard, white ceramic made from highly refined clay and a thoroughly pulverized stone containing feldspar and quartz. It was fired at even higher temperatures, ranging from 1,300 to 1,500 degrees centigrade. Porcelain is predominantly white throughout and frequently translucent. Porcelain ware, when struck sharply with a light hard object, produces a clear bell-like resonance.

For many centuries, the secrets of porcelain were known only to the Chinese. Some writers claimed that porcelain was first produced during the Han 漢 dynasty, in the second century B.C. However, no authentic porcelain from before the Sung 宋 dynasty (960–1274) has yet been discovered. The word "porcelain" itself is derived from the Portuguese, who compared porcelain to the smooth cowrie shell which they called *porzella*.

Porcelain was made from two naturally occurring minerals. One was the pure white clay called *kaolin* 高嶺土, named after a hill, Kao Lin, where the clay was found. The other mineral was *petunse* 白墩子, a hard rock containing feldspar and quartz. Kaolin was referred to as china clay and petunse as china stone. Both minerals were refined separately and made into a fine powder by pounding and grinding them in water.

Kaolin has a very high melting point and does not melt or fuse at the highest heat produced in a kiln. In contrast, petunse has a lower melting point, and it melts and fuses with the kaolin in the high heat of the kiln. The melting causes it to vitrify and acquire a glassy appearance.

The Chinese referred to the nonfusible kaolin as the "porcelain bones" and the fusible petunse as the "porcelain flesh." The quality of the porcelain depends on the proportions of the two ingredients. In fine porcelain, the proportions of petunse and kaolin are about equal. In a medium-quality product, the proportions are approximately 60 percent petunse and 40 percent kaolin.

The porcelain capital of China is the town of Ching-Te-Chen 景德鎮 in Kiangsi 江西 province, near the source of the two minerals kaolin and petunse. Archaeological finds in this area suggest that a pottery center existed near this town as early as the first century A.D. During the period of the Six Dynasties 六朝 (265–518), Ching-Te-Chen received imperial orders to produce pottery for the court. The town grew considerably during the Tang 唐 dynasty (618–906) when tea drinking swept through China, increasing the demand for teapots, cups and saucers. Ching-Te-Chen received its present name during the Sung dynasty when the court commissioned the town to produce porcelain for its use. In 1369, the first Ming 明 emperor, Hung Wu 洪武, reserved kilns in Ching-Te-Chen for the production of porcelain exclusively for the court. Following that precedent, the Ming and the Ching 清 emperors also had their porcelain made in the imperial kilns of the town.

Through the centuries, an enormous amount of imperfect and broken pottery accumulated in Ching-Te-Chen. These shards were used to pave the roads of the town. The supply of kaolin and petunse is now depleted in Ching-Te-Chen, but the two minerals are brought in from elsewhere and the kilns are still active.

The Sung dynasty is generally considered to be the first great age of porcelain, followed by the Ming and the Ching. During the Sung dynasty, porcelain was exported to Southeast Asia and to other countries in the western Pacific. During the Ming dynasty (1368–1644), Chinese porcelain reached as far as Europe and was highly prized by European aristocrats. Palaces in Europe still have their special "porcelain rooms" where the royal collections are displayed. With each succeeding period the glazes of Chinese porcelain improved in quality and the decorative motifs became more intricate.

Celadon, a beautiful green porcelain made to resemble jade, was not only admired by the Chinese but also highly prized in Europe. The name celadon derives from the French play *L'Astrée*, produced in 1610, in which a shepherd boy named Celadon wears ribbons that are the same color as the green jadelike porcelain.

Although there were many European attempts to make a true or hard-paste porcelain, the secret of how to use feldspar in the mixture proved elusive until 1707, when Johann Friedrich Bottger, a Berlin apothecary's apprentice, discovered the method. In 1710 the Meissen porcelain factory in Dresden, under the patronage of Augustus the Strong, King of Poland and Elector of Saxony, produced the first true porcelain in Europe.

CHAPTER 12

Bamboo and Jade

Bamboo

The Chinese were the first to appreciate the beauty and usefulness of bamboo, one of the world's most extraordinary plants. From ancient times to the present, it has been used extensively and in one form or another has been an integral part of daily life in every Chinese home. Poets have long extolled this noble and versatile plant, and Chinese artists have frequently painted it, cherishing its grace and beauty.

Colonel Barrington de Fonblanque, who traveled in China, observed, "What would a poor Chinese do without bamboo? Aside from its use as a food, it provides him with thatch that covers his house, the mat upon which he sleeps, the cup from which he drinks and the chopsticks with which he eats. He irrigates his fields by means of bamboo pipes; his harvest is gathered with bamboo rakes and carried away in a bamboo basket. The mast of his junk is bamboo; so is the pole of his cart. He is flogged with a bamboo cane, tortured with bamboo stakes and finally, strangled with a bamboo rope."

The antiquity of the use of bamboo in China is well established. Around 6000 B.C., a bamboo motif was used to decorate the neolithic pottery of the Yangshao 仰韶 culture. Bamboo baskets woven about 2000 B.C. have been discovered, as well as slips of bamboo which the Chinese used as a writing surface prior to the invention of paper. These bamboo slips date from the Warring States 戰國 period (475–221 B.C.).

Bamboo is actually a type of grass found all over the world in the tropic and temperate zones. It is indigenous to every continent except Europe and North America. Botanists claim there are 1,250 species of bamboo and have classified them into approximately 50 genera that vary considerably in size, shape, color and growth pattern. Some types of bamboo are only a few inches in height. Others tower to a height exceeding 150 feet and have a diameter of one foot. The colors, which may be solid or mottled, range from yellow through all shades of green to black.

Although a few types of bamboo are solid, most are hollow. The woody stem of the plant is called the culm, and it is divided by walled septa called nodes. Most of the culms are round but some are square. Interestingly, the culm does not expand its girth on growth. The new

Bamboo

shoot emerges from the ground in its full diameter. The growth rate of bamboo varies a great deal. Some types of bamboo grow amazingly fast, as much as four feet in a twenty-four-hour period, prompting the claim by some that they can hear bamboo growing.

Compared to tree timber, bamboo grows and matures much more quickly. The growing period is about one-half to two-thirds that of ordinary timber. Some types of bamboo are ready for harvest within four to six years, and the yield is high, producing up to thirty tons of bamboo per hectare. A hectare is 10,000 square meters or 2.47 acres.

Bamboo can be classified according to its growth pattern, which is either sympodial or monopodial. Bamboo with the sympodial growth pattern grows in clumps and expands outward from the periphery. The monopodial growth pattern is one in which runners or rhizomes are sent out underground in all directions before the shoots emerge from the ground. In some species, the rhizomes extend for over one hundred yards before the shoots pop up through the soil, appearing here and there in no particular pattern. Generally, bamboo with the sympodial growth pattern is found in the tropics, while bamboo with the monopodial growth pattern is found in the temperate zones.

Most people are not aware that bamboo plants flower. This happens infrequently, at intervals of 30 to 60 years, or even 120 years. When flowering takes place, all the bamboo of that species throughout the world bloom at about the same time. The flowers resemble drooping heads of wheat. After flowering, the plant dies. Later, new bamboo grows from the seeds of the flowers. In 1984 the Arrow bamboo flowered and died. As a result, the giant pandas in China that feed primarily on Arrow bamboo were threatened with starvation.

China has some four hundred species of bamboo. It is estimated that the bamboo covers an aggregate area of over 20,000 square kilometers, most of it in southern China. This comprises one-fifth of the bamboo in the world.

Bamboo is light, stiff, strong and straight-grained. It is resilient and can readily spring back into position after bending. The strength-to-weight ratio is high. These characteristics make bamboo very versatile and highly valuable.

There are over a thousand uses for bamboo. G. R. G. Worcester, discussing "Sails and

Sweeps in China," catalogued the use of bamboo by the ingenious junkmen of China and came up with the following items: "ropes, tholepins, masts, sails, net floats, basket fish-traps, awnings, food baskets, beds, blinds, bottles, bridges, brooms, foot rulers, food, lanterns, umbrellas, fans, brushes, buckets, chairs, chopsticks, combs, cooking gear, cups, drogues, dust pans, paper, pen, nails, pillows, tobacco pipes, boat hoods, anchors, fishing nets, fishing rods, flag poles, hats, ladders, lamps, musical instruments, mats, tubs, caulking material, scoops, shoes, stools, tables, tallies, tokens, torches, rat traps, flea traps, joss sticks and back scratchers."

Visitors to East Asia are often surprised to see bamboo scaffoldings used in the construction of buildings. They marvel that bamboo scaffolds can be used in the construction of skyscrapers. The reason is that bamboo is light, strong and resilient, and does not retain much heat when exposed to the hot sun.

Many bridges in China, some extending up to 300 feet, are made with bamboo and without the use of iron or nails. Bamboo is preferred instead of hemp for cable because it is stronger on a straight pull, lighter and can withstand severe friction. Experts have estimated that the working stress of bamboo cable lines exceeds 10,000 pounds per square inch.

All in all, no living thing has had as many varied uses as the versatile bamboo. The Chinese considered it to be one of the four noble plants, along with the plum, the orchid and the chrysanthemum. Because of its durability, and because it grows vigorously during the cold winter, bamboo was one of the symbols of longevity. In addition, the bamboo, the pine tree and the plum tree—trees that thrive in the cold—were considered the "Three Friends of Winter" 歲寒三友. In this group, the bamboo represents the Buddha, the pine tree Confucius, and the plum tree Lao Tzu. Collectively they symbolize happiness and good fortune.

Jade

Among all the rare metals and gems, jade has been considered by the Chinese to be the earth's most precious treasure. Through the long span of China's history, jade has had a special significance in ceremonies, religious rituals, art, literature and philosophy. The Chinese word for jade is *yu* 玉, suggesting that it is pure, precious and noble. The ancient *Record of Rites* 禮記 found specific virtues in the qualities of jade: benevolence in its gleaming surface, knowledge in its luminosity, uprightness in its unyieldingness, power in its harmlessness, purity of soul in its rarity and spotlessness, and eternity in its durability.

The Chinese believed that jade contains the positive yang 陽 principle, allowing it to overcome the negative yin 陰 principle in the earth. This quality of jade was believed to preserve the body after death, preventing the corpse from deterioration or decay. Taoist philosophers maintained that drinking a mixture of powdered jade and certain herbs conferred immortality. In a similar vein, personal ornaments, charms and amulets made of jade were believed to possess talismanic powers that protected the wearer from physical harm, insured good health, brought good luck and warded off evil spirits.

Although demonstrating a high degree of artistry, the Chinese were not the only jade carvers in the world. Jade was carved in

Mexico, Central America and South America long before the arrival of Columbus in 1492, and by the Maoris of New Zealand prior to the arrival of Captain James Cook in 1769. The first Europeans to discover the hard stone were Spanish explorers in Mexico, who brought it back to Europe and gave it the name *jada*, meaning flanks or loins. This curious name for the stone stemmed from the belief that jade had certain therapeutic properties. It was thought that wearing a piece of jade next to the skin at the flanks or loins cured kidney ailments.

By strict definition, only nephrite and jadeite are jade. These two stones differ in many respects, including chemical composition, structure, properties, areas of deposit and uses. The word nephrite is derived from the Greek word *nephros*, meaning kidney. Nephrite was always considered by the Chinese to be the true jade 眞玉 or soft jade 軟玉. A silicate of calcium and magnesium, nephrite is microfibrous, difficult to fracture and almost soapy in appearance. It is one of the toughest minerals in the world, second only to the black diamond, because of its fibrous structure and hardness. In fact, fifty tons of pressure are needed to crush one cubic inch of nephrite. Since the black diamond is used only for industrial purposes, nephrite is considered the toughest gemstone.

The ancient Chinese used only nephrite in their ceremonies and rituals. However, there is no evidence that nephrite was ever mined within the provinces of China proper. The chief sources of nephrite were Khotan 干闐 and areas close to the Kun Lun mountains 崑崙山 in the remote western region of Chinese Turkestan, now called Sinkiang 新疆. Other nephrite deposits have been found in Siberia, the south island of New Zealand, Alaska, British Columbia, Wyoming and along the beaches of California from Crescent City in the north to San Diego in the south. The nephrite mines in and near Khotan have been almost depleted, and the quality of jade found there in recent years is poor. The Chinese now depend on jadeite from Burma.

Jadeite is a relatively new stone for the Chinese. It has been used extensively only since 1784, when large quantities were first imported from Burma. In contrast to soft jade or nephrite, the new stone was called hard jade 硬玉 by the Chinese. In 1863, the French scientist Alexis Damour, finding that the hard stone similar to jade found in Burma was not nephrite, named it jadeite. As a silicate of sodium and aluminum, jadeite is microgranular in structure. Because it is granular, it fractures more easily than nephrite and is more brilliant when polished.

The most highly prized color for jadeite is a rich imperial or emerald green. Pure jadeite, however, is white, as is pure nephrite. Other colors come from the presence of additional minerals in the stone, especially iron, manganese and chromium. Iron oxides and iron silicates produce the largest variety of hues, ranging from pale green, yellow, brown and blue to black. Manganese salts produce the various shades of gray and pink, and it is the presence of chromium that causes jade to be green.

In China, jade was for both the living and the dead. It was probably first used to fashion weapons and tools. Later it was carved into emblems of official rank and power. A flat oblong slab of jade with a hole at one end, called *kuei* 圭, was used as a scepter indicating imperial power and authority. A cylindrical hole within a square tube of jade, called *tsung* 琮, symbolized Earth, and a flat disc with a hole in the center, called *pi* 璧, was the symbol of

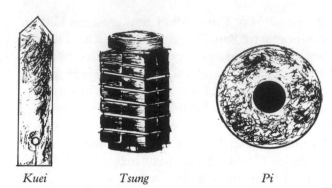

Kuei   *Tsung*   *Pi*

Heaven. The width of the hole in the *pi* was usually one-fifth of the diameter of the disc. The emperor, the Son of Heaven, consulted Heaven through the medium of the *pi*.

Only royalty of the first rank was permitted to use the finest jade in ceremonies and as adornments of their court attire. Winners of contests of skill were awarded a jade scepter while those who placed second earned a gold scepter and those who placed third, an ivory scepter.

Many everyday articles were made from jade, such as tassel weights for draperies, robes and pouches; musical instruments like chimes and flutes; handles and guards for knives and swords, girdles, buckles, belt hooks, censers, statues, ornaments, chopsticks, saucers and bowls. Scholars used jade paperweights, seals, writing-brush handles and penholders. Jade jewelry such as bracelets, rings, combs, hairpins, earrings, necklaces, pendants, brooches, charms and amulets were worn not only for personal adornment but also as talismans.

Funerary jade pieces were used as articles for worship and for the soul's use in the next world. Ritual jade pieces were entombed with the corpse to provide the soul with suitable equipment for worship. Jade wine vessels, bowls, plates, cups, saucers and replicas of ser-

vants, horses, chariots, houses and so on were placed in tombs to provide a degree of comfort in the life after death.

It was written that "jade cannot prevent the living from dying but it can prevent the corpse from decaying." Toward this end, jade was placed on and around the dead body in a strictly prescribed manner. Jade pieces were used to plug the nine orifices, and a jade cicada carving was often placed on the tongue along with rice. The cicada was considered an emblem of immortality because the insect larva passes the first four years of its life underground, then sheds its skin and emerges from the ground as a mature insect.

Ancient records suggested that Han 漢 dynasty emperors and royalty were buried in jade suits. It was not until June 1968 that archaeologists from the Chinese Academy of Sciences made one of the most sensational discoveries of the century in Hopei 河北 province. They found two tombs, each containing a jade burial suit. Research revealed that the partially fragmented burial suit lying on the floor of the first tomb was the shroud of Prince Liu Sheng 劉勝, a carefree, fun-loving and irresponsible king, who died in 141 B.C. The jade burial suit found in the second tomb belonged to his consort, Princess Tou Wan 竇綰.

In addition, more than 2,800 funerary articles made of jade, bronze, gold and silver as well as various types of pottery and silks were found in the tombs. The two jade burial suits, however, were the most spectacular finds. Prince Liu Sheng's burial suit was made from more than 2,690 pieces of green jade. The smallest piece measured 1.5 by 1 cm., and the largest piece 4.5 by 3.5 cm. The thickness of the jade varied from 0.2 to 0.35 cm. Each piece of jade had four holes, one in each corner, so that they could be sewn together with fine quality gold threads,

Jade burial suit of Liu Sheng

totalling 1,110 grams. The suit was flexible and consisted of 12 sections that fitted closely around the corpse.

The exact date of Princess Tou Wan's death is unknown but it was some years after the prince's death. Her jade burial suit was similar in construction but consisted of fewer pieces: 2,156 in total and 703 grams of gold thread. The pieces covering her torso were brownish jade with X-shaped markings.

The jade suits designed to preserve the bodies of the prince and princess after death failed to accomplish their purpose. The two bodies had been reduced to dust long before the archaeologists uncovered the tombs. Now restored, the two jade burial suits are a main attraction at the Palace Museum in Peking's Forbidden City. There can be little doubt that although the Chinese were not the only people to carve jade, the art of jade carving was perfected in China.

Actually, the terms "jade carving" and "carved jade" are something of a misnomer. Jade is so hard that it cannot be carved with metal tools, not even with high-grade steel tools. The only method of working it is to grind away the unwanted portions with an abrasive that is harder. This is a tedious and painstaking operation, requiring months and even years to complete the carving of an intricate jade piece. Early jadesmiths used tubular bamboo grinders and strings moistened with fine, wet sand as an abrasive to grind and cut the jade. Later metal tips were added to the grinders. A special notched-wire saw replaced the string that had been used to cut the jade. Now power tools have replaced the bamboo grinder and saw.

In jade carving, the abrasive is more important than the type of grinder. The earliest abrasive was the fine, wet sand mentioned above. Later crushed garnet and rubies came into use, although they did not totally replace sand. The next development was the use of emery, a naturally produced impure form of a very hard abrasive called corundum, which could be pulverized to a powder. Gems such as the ruby, sapphire, Oriental topaz and amethyst are all forms of pure, transparent crystalline corundum, and all varieties of corundum, emery as well as gemstones, are harder than sand and quartz. Emery, found north of the Great Wall in Siberia, was introduced into China in the twelfth century, around the time of Kublai Khan 元四祖. Since the hard emery was cheap and readily available, it soon replaced sand as the preferred abrasive for jade carving.

In 1891, silicon carbide was synthesized and marketed under the trade name of Carborundum. This compound, which is almost as hard as diamonds, is now used as an abrasive in jade carving. Although carborundum can grind away jade faster than other abrasives, faster does not always mean better. The use of carborundum and power tools reduced the degree of control by the jadesmith. On close inspection, jade carved with carborundum often reveals sharp or rough edges and tiny gouged ridges, flaws not seen when softer abrasives were used.

After the jade has been carved, it must be polished to remove sharp edges and flaws, giving the piece a smooth, soft appearance. A first polishing is done with a grinding disc or a mold made with a mixture of shellac and a fine abrasive; the disc or mold is rotated on a lathe. The final polishing is done with leather buffers and a paste made of a fine abrasive mixed with loess, a chalky silt. The leather buffers come in different grades, shapes and sizes so that even the most inaccessible parts of the carving can be reached and polished.

The Chinese use the term jade rather loosely. It can be applied to nephrite, jadeite or any stone of great beauty. Thus, many semi-precious stones resembling jade have been sold, knowingly or unknowingly, as jade. Of the thirty to forty stones mistakenly called jade by dealers in China, Hong Kong and Taiwan, a few of the more common are:

Serpentine (Soochou Jade). This stone is very similar to nephrite jade in appearance. It can confuse even a good jeweler on casual inspection.

Aventurine (Indian Jade). Aventurine is a form of quartz and has a glassy appearance. It is not a very expensive stone.

Chrysoprase (Australian Jade). This stone is similar to agate. It has a uniform green color and is often mistaken for jadeite.

A novice buying expensive jade jewelry or investing in antique jade should bear in mind the following precautions: Be sure the stone is genuine nephrite or jadeite. Well-carved quality jade is expensive—beware of bargains. To ensure authenticity, buy only from knowledgeable and reputable merchants.

CHAPTER 13

Chinese Food

The Chinese have been extremely preoccupied with food for centuries. Both the poor farmer and the wealthy official, the illiterate laborer and the educated scholar have paid inordinate attention to the preparation and enjoyment of food. One indication of the special place of food in the consciousness of the Chinese is the common greeting "Have you eaten?" It is also commonplace for guests at a dinner to discuss freely the ingredients, the preparation and the taste of the various dishes served.

Regional Cooking

Foods and methods of preparation vary considerably in different regions of China. Although there is no unanimity on the classification of the types of regional cooking, they can generally be described in terms of four major regions—the north, the east, the south and the west. Each region's cooking can be further subdivided into the types of cooking associated with different provinces and cities.

Northern or Peking cooking has been greatly influenced by the Moslems, Mongolians and Manchurians. These minority races brought in

lamb and beef dishes. People in the north eat more wheat than rice because the northern plains are better suited for wheat cultivation. Wheat is used to make buns, pancakes and noodles. Northern dishes tend to be spicy and oily.

Eastern or Shanghai cooking is noted for its seafood—the fish, shrimp, prawns, crabs and other seafood varieties that are found in great abundance in the eastern coastal provinces. People in this area eat more rice than wheat. The mild climate, fertile soil and plentiful water supply from the Yangtze River 揚子江 make the area well suited for growing crops and cultivating rice in wet paddies. Eastern cooking is noted for its sweet-and-sour sauces, its "red" cooking using dark soy sauce and its sumptuous casserole dishes. Oil is used in large quantities. Generally, the dishes here are not as spicy as those from the northern and western regions.

Southern cooking is famous throughout China, especially Cantonese cooking from the capital of Kwangtung 廣東 province. The main staple is rice. Southern dishes use many tropical vegetables and products from the sea. Cantonese cooking attempts to bring out the natural food flavors through the use of lightly seasoned sauces. Vegetables are cooked rapidly so that they retain their crispness. Cooking from the province of Fukien 福建 is similar to Cantonese cooking except that in Fukienese cooking there is greater use of frying and dishes have more gravy.

Western cooking comes mainly from the provinces of Szechuan 四川 and Hunan 湖南. It is noted for its liberal use of hot red peppers, ginger and garlic. Pork, beef, fish, fowl and noodle dishes are usually very hot and peppery.

Foodstuffs

The most popular meat in China is pork. The pig is highly valued by farmers because it eats everything, including leftovers and slop. The pig furnishes not only pork but also leather and bristles, and its excrement makes excellent fertilizer. Most peasants, in addition to farming their plots, raise a few pigs.

Beef is not as widely eaten as pork. Cattle are more useful as beasts of burden. They help the peasant plow the fields and pull the wagons. Besides, it is more economical for people to eat the grains they grow than to feed it to cattle to produce beef. Veal is seldom eaten. The Chinese feel it is wrong to slaughter a cow for food because it is regarded as the farmer's helper and friend.

Vegetables of course comprise a large part of the Chinese diet. Vegetable oils, especially peanut oil, are used for cooking rather than lard. Duck is the favorite domestic fowl, followed by chicken, squab and goose. Eggs, especially duck eggs, fresh, salted or preserved, are frequently eaten. For seafood, the Chinese relish fresh water and salt water fish, shrimp, prawns and crabs. They also eat oysters, scallops, clams, conches, squids, cuttlefish, jellyfish, sea cucumbers and sharks' fins.

Dairy products such as milk, butter and cheese do not play a significant role in the Chinese diet, except among some of the minority races. Chinese use milk occasionally as a flavoring agent and then only in limited quantities. Many Chinese, after the age of two, are unable to tolerate cow's milk, because after that age they lack the enzyme, lactase, which is needed to digest the milk sugar, lactose, present in cow's milk. For these individuals, drinking cow's milk causes abdominal pain and intestinal upsets. Chinese generally detest cheese.

Food Preservation

Throughout its history, China has been frequently plagued with floods, droughts and other natural calamities. To guard against the possibility of starvation and famines, people had to preserve food in times of plenty.

Various methods of preserving food were developed, including drying, salting, sugaring, steeping, pickling, soaking foods in oils and smoking. A partial list of the foods preserved with these methods would include grains, vegetables, fruits, algae, seaweeds, fungi, meats, poultry, eggs and many kinds of seafood.

Cooking Methods

Many methods are employed in Chinese cooking. The main techniques are stir frying, light shallow frying, deep frying, simmering, boiling, steaming, stewing, sizzling, roasting, smoking and baking.

Kitchen Utensils

The Chinese have developed some distinctive kitchen utensils, including the wok 鑊, the cleaver 菜刀, the chopping block 砧板, the steamer tray 蒸籠, the bamboo-handled wire net strainer 笊籬 and of course the chopsticks 筷子.

The wok is a deep, thin round metal cooking pan with a rounded bottom and flared sides. It is made of malleable cast iron, copper, aluminum or stainless steel. The best woks are made with cast iron. A new cast iron wok must be seasoned with cooking oil before it is used. The wok is extremely fuel efficient. Intense heat can be concentrated at the rounded bottom, making it ideal for rapid stir frying. Oil and sauces gravitate to the bottom and easily mix with the food during the cooking process. The wok is versatile and can be used for stir frying, light shallow frying, deep frying, simmering, boiling, steaming and braising. The rounded bottom also makes it easy to clean.

Chopping block and cleaver

The cleaver is an all-purpose knife. It has a cylindrical wooden handle and a broad rectangular blade made with soft but tough steel. The relatively soft steel blade is easy to sharpen but must be dried after washing to prevent rusting. The cleaver is used for slicing, shred-

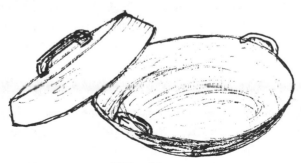

Wok with cover

Bamboo steamer trays

ding, scoring, dicing, mincing and chopping. Because of its weight, it can easily chop through bone and hard shellfish. The butt and the back of the blade are used for pounding and mashing. The flat of the blade is used for crushing and smashing ginger and garlic, and for transferring the cut food from the chopping block to the plate or bowl.

The cleaver requires a heavy, hard and tough chopping block, preferably one made from certain kinds of fruit trees. The best chopping block is made from the log of a tamarind 酸子 tree. The next best are made from a longan 龍眼 tree or a litchee 荔枝 tree. For general home use, the chopping block is usually about three to four inches thick and fifteen inches in diameter.

The steamer tray is made from bamboo or metal. The bamboo tray is latticed at the bottom. A metal tray made from aluminum or stainless steel is perforated at the bottom. The openings at the bottom of the tray allow the hot steam to enter and cook the food.

The bamboo-handled wire net strainer is a multipurpose kitchen utensil, especially when cooking with a wok. It is used to remove foods from boiling water and hot oil. It can be used as a colander to drain off liquids and rinse foods.

Chopsticks are Chinese in origin and were thought to date from the third century B.C. until three pairs of chopsticks were found in a Shang 商 dynasty burial site. This means that chopsticks were in use in China before the eleventh century B.C.

Chopsticks have been made from wood, bamboo, silver, gold, ivory, coral, jade, and recently, from plastics. Chopsticks used for eating average about ten inches in length. Generally, the top half is about one-fourth of an inch thick and squared. The lower half is rounded and slightly tapered. Chopsticks used for cooking are longer and thicker than those used for eating, and must be made from wood or bamboo, which can withstand high heat, do not warp, do not conduct heat and do not alter the taste of food in cooking. Cooking chopsticks are used for beating eggs, piercing meat, mixing sauce, stir frying, straining and removing foods from hot oils and liquids.

To be eaten with chopsticks, food must be cut into bite-size pieces in the kitchen. With a little experience, one can easily manipulate the chopsticks and, if necessary, separate meat from the bone or shrimp from the shell with one's teeth and without use of the fingers. In Chinese etiquette it is considered perfectly proper to raise the rice bowl to the mouth and shovel the rice into the mouth with chopsticks. A plate, however, is never raised to the mouth from the table.

Wire net strainer

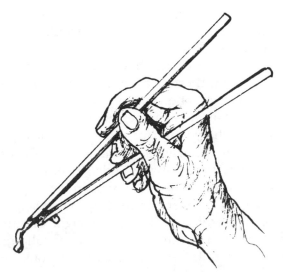

Proper method of holding chopsticks

Many people, Chinese included, use chopsticks incorrectly. The proper method is to hold one stick stationary and move the other. With the fingers of the right hand curved comfortably, the stationary stick is placed at the angle between the thumb and index finger and at the thumb-side of the ring finger at the distal segment. Slight thumb pressure is exerted to stabilize the stick. The movable stick is held like a pencil. This stick is placed between the tips of the index and middle fingers and is held in place with the thumb. To open and close the chopsticks, the index and middle fingers are raised and lowered.

The Chinese word for "chopsticks" has an interesting derivation. The characters for "eating sticks" are 筷子. The characters for "fast or nimble child" are 快子. Both terms are pronounced exactly the same, *kuai tzu*. The character *kuai* 筷 in "eating sticks" is written with a bamboo radical ⺮ while the character *kuai* 快 meaning "fast" is written without the bamboo radical. Westerners mistakenly thought the word chopsticks meant fast or nimble child. Since the pidgin English term for fast was "chop chop," we now have the word chopsticks.

The Chinese regard chopsticks with great respect. Children are not allowed to use them as drumsticks, and women do not use them to adorn their hair. Chopsticks are never used to strike the bowl, plate or cup to attract attention because that is a gesture used by beggars to solicit food and alms.

Rice

During the neolithic period, the chief grain of the people living along the Yellow River 黃河 was millet. They may have planted some wheat as well. At the same time, some of the minority races in the far south were probably planting rice in dry fields. Millet and wheat remained the principal grains in China through the Tang 唐 dynasty (618–906). Since that time, rice gradually became more prominent in the Chinese diet. This was especially true in the south where there was adequate water and rainfall to provide paddies for the cultivation of the long-grained "wet rice" that had come from an area near the Bay of Bengal in India.

According to the Rice Council of America, there are more than forty thousand varieties of rice grown in the world today, varying in size, shape, texture, taste and color. The color of rice can range from white through ivory, yellow, brown and red to black. In the United States only four varieties of rice are cultivated. They are the long-grain, medium-grain, short-grain and glutinous rice. The long-grain rice, *Oryza indica*, is known as Louisiana, Patina or Indian rice. When cooked, this rice is fluffy, firm and less inclined to stick together. Chinese prefer the long-grain rice because they like the firm texture and consider it to be tastier. It is the best rice to accompany Chinese dishes. The firmness and lack of cohesiveness make it ideal for preparing Chinese fried rice. The medium-grain rice is a little shorter and a bit more tender than the long-grain rice. It is used to make Western rice desserts. The short-grain rice, *Oryza japonica*, is known as Japanese or California rice. This rice, shorter than the medium-grain rice, is soft in texture and more inclined to stick together after cooking. As its name suggests, this rice is favored by the Japanese. The stickiness of the cooked rice is more suitable for preparing *sushi*, a Japanese delicacy which is a small ball of rice molded in the palm of the hand and topped, usually, with a slice of raw seafood.

Glutinous rice 糯米 is called "sticky rice." The Japanese call it *mochi* rice because the pounded cooked glutinous rice is used to prepare *mochi*, a soft, chewy confection. Glutinous rice is short, opaque and pearly white in appearance. It can be used as a whole grain or pounded into flour. If used as a whole grain, it must be washed and soaked before cooking. Cooked glutinous rice is very sticky. The Chinese use glutinous rice to make a sweet porridge 粥, stuffings for chicken and duck dishes, a rice pudding wrapped in bamboo leaves called *tsung* 粽, puffed rice cakes 通米 and a banquet dessert called Eight Precious Rice 八寶飯. This special dessert is made with glutinous rice mixed with eight other ingredients including lotus seeds, almond seeds and slices of red jujubes 紅棗, and sweetened with several candied fruits, sweet bean paste and brown syrup. Also, fermented cooked glutinous rice is used to make rice wine. Flour from glutinous rice is used to make pastries such as puddings 糕, dumplings and deep fried stuffed round "doughnuts" 煎堆.

The Chinese do not have a general term for rice. Instead, there is a specific term for every stage of growth and type of rice product. *Miao* 苗, for instance, is the germinating rice plant, *yang* 秧 is the young rice shoot used for planting, *ho* 禾 is the growing plant, *ku* 穀 is the unhusked rice, *mi* 米 is the hulled rice, *fan* 飯 is cooked rice and *chou* 粥 is rice porridge.

Rice is an excellent grain. It is low in sodium and cholesterol, and it contains eight essential amino acids and vitamins. Rice is nonallergic, easily digestible, easy to cook, delicious and reasonably priced.

Rice, when served, must not be pressed into the bowl. Only beggars do that, so that more rice can be served in a bowl. Parents in China teach their children never to waste rice. Every grain in the rice bowl must be eaten because this all-important grain is only produced through considerable back-breaking labor.

Soybeans

Chinese refer to the soybean, *Glycine max*, as the "big bean" 大豆 or the "yellow bean" 黃豆. It is the most important legume cultivated in China. Archaeologists have found soybeans dating from the Spring and Summer 春秋 era (770–475 B.C.).

Soybeans play an important role in the Chinese diet. They yield more protein per acre than any other food crop and are the chief source of protein for people whose diets are generally deficient in animal and fish protein. The protein-rich soybean can even be considered the "botanical cow" of China. A pound of soybeans has twice the protein of a pound of beef. In fact, pound for pound, the soybean is considered the richest of all foods in protein. Furthermore, a pound of dried soybeans contains more iron than a pound of beef liver, and three times the thiamine and six times the riboflavin found in brown rice. Soybean milk, moreover, is richer in digestible calcium than the equivalent amount of cow's milk.

Soybeans are eaten in many ways. They can be boiled and eaten as a snack, eaten as sprouts or ground into a meal. Soybean sprouts 豆芽 are different from ordinary bean sprouts 芽菜, which are sprouts from the mung bean 綠豆. The bean leaves of soybean sprouts are much larger than those of bean sprouts and have a nutty texture and flavor. The bean sprouts with small bean leaves have more of a vegetable texture. Salted black beans 豆豉 are soybeans that have been fermented and salted. These pungent beans are used to season fish, shellfish, pork, beef and chicken dishes. Wet ground soybeans are used to make soybean milk and bean curds, and soybeans and soybean flour are used to manufacture soy sauce.

Soybean Milk and Bean Curds

One method of making soybean milk, bean curds and related products begins with soaking the dry uncooked soybeans in water. The softened beans are then ground in water to form a thick fluid. The finer the beans are ground, the smoother the texture of the product. After grinding, the slurry or thick semisolid fluid is diluted with water and strained. The dregs of the soybeans 豆渣 are fed to chickens and pigs or used as food by the poor. The raw soybean solution is then cooked.

Soybean milk 豆漿 is the cooked soybean solution. This cooked solution resembles cow's milk and is usually drunk after it has been seasoned with sugar or condiments. When the soybean solution is heated to a certain temperature, a "skin" or a film like that of boiled milk forms on the surface. The film 腐皮 is skimmed and used either fresh or dried. The dried skimmed film is made either in sheets or rolled into sticks 腐竹.

The addition of a coagulant to the cooked soybean solution causes the protein to precipitate. A common coagulant is gypsum, which is calcium sulfate. The watery semisolid precipitates are the bean curds or *tou fu* 豆腐. The watery bean curds, resembling soft custard, are called "bean curd flower" 豆腐花 and can be eaten either fresh with soy sauce and other condiments or lightly stir fried. The consistency of the soft watery bean curds can be altered, and curds of different firmness produced, by pressing and drying. The relatively firm dry bean curds are called "dry *tou fu*" 豆腐乾. Firmer bean curds can be stir fried, deep fried, stuffed or added to soups.

Bean curds fermented with rice wine is called "Chinese cheese" 腐乳. It is yellowish in color and resembles soft cheese in texture and flavor. "Southern cheese" 南乳 is made from fermented bean curds seasoned with red spices. These fermented bean curds are used mainly for seasoning.

Soy Sauce

Soy sauce, called *shih yu* 豉油 by southern Chinese and *chiang yu* 醬油 by northern Chinese, is one of the world's oldest flavoring agents. It is used extensively in East Asian cooking.

The process of manufacturing soy sauce begins with fermenting a mixture of soybean flour or soybeans, a lightly ground grain such as wheat or barley and a yeast. The yeast is *Aspergillus oryzae*, *Aspergillus soyae* or a similar yeast. The resulting fluid is then brined and re-fermented with the same starter yeast and *lactobacillus*, a bacteria that ferments sugar. The fluid is then strained and bottled. The process of fermentation and aging can be quite long, up to eighteen months for some types of soy sauce.

Basically, there are three types of Chinese soy sauce—light, dark and heavy. The light soy sauce 生抽 is the most commonly used. This sauce contains sugar and has a fine delicate flavor. It is used as a dipping condiment and in cooking when its flavor and light color are desired. Dark soy sauce 老抽 contains caramel, a form of burnt sugar. It is darker, thicker and richer than light soy sauce. Although it can be used as a dipping condiment, dark soy sauce is used primarily in "red" cooking for its dark color and full-bodied flavor. Heavy soy sauce 滴珠油 contains molasses and is very thick. This type of soy sauce has a sweet-salty flavor and is used in basting and for making dark brown sauces.

The term *shoyu* is a generic name for Japanese soy sauce. Japanese soy sauces are different from those of China and Korea. One of the ingredients used in making *shoyu* is malt. In taste, it is between the Chinese light and dark soy sauces. *Shoyu* made in America can be produced in about twenty-four hours with the aid of chemicals and tends to be salty and bitter. Fastidious Chinese feel that Japanese soy sauce lacks the delicate flavor found in Chinese light soy sauce.

Worcestershire sauce, a piquant sauce originally made in Worcester, England, is a modified soy sauce. Essentially, it is soy sauce altered by the addition of vinegar, anchovies, tamarind, onions, garlic, shallots and other spices and flavorings.

Tea

There is no unanimity regarding the origin of the tea plant in China. Some believe that tea was drunk in Szechuan province before the Han 漢 dynasty (206 B.C.–A.D. 220). Others maintain that the tea plant is not indigenous to China and was introduced by a monk from northern India in the sixth century. The difference of opinion may be owing to the fact that there are two species of tea plants, both related to the camellia. The two species are the Chinese tea plant, *Thea chinesis*, and the Indian tea plant, *Thea assamica*. The tea plants in China today are probably hybrids of these two species.

There is general agreement, however, that the best teas are produced in the southern provinces of China. Tea is grown in the mountainous regions of Chekiang 浙江, Anhui 安徽, Fukien 福建, Kwangtung 廣東, Szechuan 四川 and Yunnan 雲南 provinces. The Chinese call the infusion of tea leaves *cha* 茶. The term "tea" was derived from the Fukienese, who called it *tay* instead of *cha*.

Tea drinking in China gradually spread from the south to the north. Widespread tea drinking began during the Tang dynasty, sometime between the eighth and tenth centuries. It then extended from China to her neighboring countries. Buddhist monks introduced tea to Japan in the thirteen century. The Mongolians, who now drink copious amounts of tea, ignored it until after the fourteenth century. Tea was brought to Europe by the Dutch at the close of the sixteenth century.

Tea leaves are hand picked. The best leaves

come from the first picking, when the leaves are in the budding stage. The more mature leaves that are harvested later and located farther down from the tips of the branches are not as good for making tea.

Fresh tea leaves are not aromatic. The tea fragrance emerges after the leaves are cured slowly under low heat. The cured tea leaves are either black or green depending on whether the leaves are fermented or unfermented. The cured unfermented leaves are grayish green and the cured fermented leaves are brownish black. Chinese, however, do not classify tea according to the color of the cured leaves. Tea is generally classified green or red according to the color of the brewed tea.

Green tea 青茶 is made from unfermented leaves, which are usually young and tender. The tea is light greenish gold, delicate with a pleasing bouquet and refreshing. Red tea 紅茶 is made from fully fermented tea leaves. Usually the mature, coarser leaves are gathered and fermented in a moist atmosphere. After fermentation, the leaves are cured. The tea is reddish, full-bodied, stronger in flavor, and pleasantly pungent. A variant of red tea is tea brewed from semifermented leaves. The partially fermented leaves produce a straw-amber tea that combines the body of red tea with the delicate bouquet of green tea. This tea goes well with heavy Chinese foods.

Tea leaves can also be scented with various flowers and fruits. Some of the flowers used for this purpose are chrysanthemum, jasmine and rose. A commonly used fruit is litchee 荔枝.

There are approximately 250 varieties of tea with prices ranging from a few cents to several hundred dollars a pound. The most popular teas are the unfermented green teas and the semifermented red teas. Dragon Well 龍井 tea, produced in the region of Dragon Well near the city of Hangchow 杭州, is considered the finest green tea. One of the most popular semifermented red teas is Dark Dragon 烏龍 tea. The Iron Goddess of Mercy 鐵觀音 tea is the most famous fully fermented red tea. This tea, when properly brewed, is rich, thick and pungent, and it is usually served in little tea cups.

The Chinese generally brew their tea in porcelain ware, either in a porcelain teapot or in a porcelain cup with a lid. The utensils used in preparing tea must be clean and not washed with soap or detergent. The cup or teapot is usually prewarmed with hot water. Freshly drawn water heated to the boiling point is then poured over the tea leaves which have been placed in the cup or teapot. The tea leaves are brewed for about three to five minutes without stirring to bring out the full flavor before drinking. Tea leaves should not be boiled. Water that is not heated to the boiling point or boiled too long will alter the fragrance and flavor of the tea.

In the home, tea is kept warm for long periods by placing the porcelain teapot in a padded basket called a tea caddy. Chinese tea is fragrant, pleasant and refreshing; cream and sugar are not needed to enhance its flavor. Tea taken before meals cleanses the palate. During meals, it goes well with Chinese food, and after meals, it refreshes the palate. According to the *Catalogue of Native Herbs* 本草綱目, "the action of tea on the body system has never been considered to be anything but beneficial. Tea clears the voice, gives brilliancy to the eyes, opens up the avenues of the body, promotes digestion, removes flatulence and regulates body temperature."

In China, moreover, the universal drinking of tea brewed with boiling water has saved the lives of millions of people. Because the water supply is usually contaminated with harmful bacteria and parasites, the practice of boiling water for tea has prevented numerous gastrointestinal diseases and parasitic infestations.

Edible Bird's Nests

For more than ten centuries, the Chinese have prized the edible nests of the *Collocalia francica* 燕窩 as a rare delicacy. Although commonly called a swallow, this bird is actually a small swiftlet that lives only in a few limited areas of Thailand, Indonesia, Malaysia, Vietnam and the Philippines. People who collect their nests protect their territories jealously. Intruders who come near or poachers who infringe on the area are greeted with hostility and risk being killed for trespassing.

Collecting the nests is an extremely dangerous occupation, for they are found in pitch-black, bat-infested sea caves that are sometimes as high as three hundred feet above sea level. Like bats, the swiftlets emit sounds while flying and the echoes enable them to navigate and find their nests in the dark caves. The collector climbs a bamboo-rattan scaffold carrying a lantern or a flashlight and a special tool used for gently grasping and loosening the nests that are firmly glued to the cave walls. The collected nests are placed in a rattan basket attached to a pulley and slowly lowered to the ground.

The nests resemble shallow half-cups and are made from a gelatinous substance secreted from the swollen salivary glands of the male bird. The secretion is ejected on the cave wall and left to dry and harden. Many layers are added until the nest is completed.

The birds built three nests a year beginning in January. The first completed nests are collected in late February or March. The second nests are collected in April or May. The third nests are left undisturbed so that the birds can reproduce and bring up a new generation of birds.

To the Chinese, these edible bird's nests are not only delicious but also valuable for maintaining good health. They believe that the bird's nests nourish the lungs, kidneys, heart, stomach and all the other organs of the body. If eaten regularly, they improve one's complexion, mental capacity, vigor and health. They are also considered a powerful aphrodisiac. The curious thing is that chemical analysis has shown that their nutritional value is minimal.

Bird's nests are bland and tasteless, but when cooked with a good soup stock, they become a delicious delicacy. Their texture, which imparts a pleasant sensation when eaten, is also part of their attraction. Serving bird's nest soup is the high point of a formal dinner and a mark of great hospitality.

Shark's Fins

The Chinese also prize shark's fins 魚翅. This rare delicacy is made from the fins of sharks found in the warm seas of the torrid zone. The edible portion of the fin is the needle-like cartilage. Although dried whole shark's fins can be purchased occasionally, they must be cleaned and processed before cooking. The more commonly sold shark's fins have been cleaned and dried, and the skin and flesh removed. What remains is only the transparent, yellowish cartilage. The processed fins are expensive and come in different grades. Top-grade fins are about five inches in length, medium-grade fins are about two to three inches and the lowest grade, or remnants, are about one inch.

The fins per se are tasteless. When cooked in a rich stock or braised with meats, they become tasty, and the crunchy texture of the fins is quite pleasant. As with the bird's nests, the Chinese believe that shark's fins are not only delicious but nutritious as well. Eating the fins is thought to improve one's strength and virility.

Incidentally, the Danish people also eat the needle-like cartilage from shark's fins. The cartilage they eat is tiny, about one-fourth to one-half inch in length, because the sharks found in the cold seas near Denmark are very small. The Danes cook the cartilage in chicken broth and their shark's fin soup is somewhat similar to the Chinese soup.

Ginkgo Nut

The Chinese originally called the nut from the ginkgo tree *yin hsing* 銀杏, or "silver apricot." Later the name was changed to *yin kuo* 銀果, or "silver fruit." Now it is called *pai kuo* 白果, or "white fruit." Ginkgo is not a Japanese name. It was derived from the older Chinese name *yin kuo.*

Ginkgo trees grew all over the world during the Jurassic period of the Mesozoic era, 150 million years ago. This was the time when huge dinosaurs roamed the earth and reptiles swam the seas and flew in the air. This was also about the time when the first birds appeared in Europe. Today all the trees of the ginkgo family have become extinct except for one species, *Ginkgo biloba.*

This species is indigenous to eastern China. It is an attractive tree with fan-shaped leaves. The fruit is fleshy and has an inner stone and kernel. The ripe fruit is yellow and has a putrid odor when the flesh is mashed.

The kernel of the ginkgo fruit is slightly bitter when cooked. It is used as an ingredient in soups, stuffings and the vegetarian dish *chai* 齋.

Chop Suey

Chop suey is unknown in China and cannot be considered a typical Chinese dish. Webster's dictionary defines chop suey as a Chinese American dish served with rice. The name was derived from the Cantonese dialect 廣州話, in which the word *tsaap* 雜 means "miscellaneous" and *sui* 碎 means "bits." So chop suey literally means "miscellaneous bits."

It is said that when Viceroy Li Hung-Chang 李鴻章, an advisor to the Manchurian throne and negotiator of the Boxer Rebellion Settlement Protocol in 1901, entertained non-Chinese guests in the United States, he instructed his Chinese chef to prepare a dinner. The chef did so not knowing how to cook Western dishes, so he concocted a dish from the leftovers in his kitchen. He used some bean sprouts, bits of pork, celery, bamboo shoots, snow peas and mushrooms. He stir fried the mixture and served it.

The guests apparently enjoyed the makeshift dish. When asked the name of the delicious dish, Li Hung-Chang replied that it was "chop suey," a dish of miscellaneous bits.

Other Foods

For people not familiar with Chinese food, many of the ingredients used seem unusual, to say the least. This has led to the remark that "the Chinese eat everything in the sky except an airplane, everything in the sea except a submarine and everything with four legs except a table.''

Some of the more exotic Chinese foods have been discussed above. Others worthy of mention, listed in alphabetical order, will conclude this chapter.

Algae 髮菜

This black hairlike algae is found only in fresh water ponds. The dried algae is used in preparing the vegetarian dish *chai* 齋. It is also used as a bedding for steamed pot roast pork 扣肉.

Bamboo Shoots 竹筍

Crisp tender bamboo shoots are used as a vegetable. They are sold fresh, dried, pickled 酸筍 or canned.

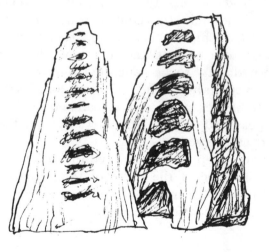

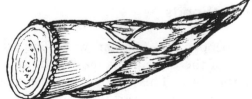

Bamboo shoots

Clams, Dried 蜆乾

Dried clams are used to flavor soups and other dishes.

Coriander 芫荽

This herb, commonly called Chinese parsley, is not indigenous to China and was probably introduced around the fifth century. The pungent aromatic leaves are used as a garnish and a flavoring agent.

Cuttlefish, Dried 墨魚

This marine mollusk is related to the squid and has a calcareous internal shell. It is used to flavor soups.

Duck, Preserved 臘鴨

The whole duck is salted in brine, cured and dried. It is often preserved in oil. Preserved duck is delicious after steaming.

Duck Egg, Preserved 皮蛋

Preserved duck egg is also called ''ancient egg,'' ''one-hundred-year-old egg'' or ''one-thousand-year-old egg.''

A misinformed national television commentator, discussing the Chinese, said that they were very patient people. They buried a duck egg for one thousand years, after which they dug it up and ate it. In reality, the duck egg is preserved with a mixture of lime, salt and ash for approximately one hundred days. After this period of time, the albumen turns amber-brown and has a consistency of firm gelatin. The yolk turns grayish-green and resembles soft cheese in texture and taste.

Preserved duck egg is delicious when eaten uncooked with a little oil, a little oyster sauce and sweet pickles. It is often served at banquets as a cold dish. The pureed preserved egg added to rice gruel 粥 makes the gruel a tasty evening snack.

Duck Egg, Salted 鹹蛋

The duck egg is salted in brine for about thirty to forty days. The albumen remains a liquid but the yolk turns firm and bright orange. In contrast to the preserved duck egg, the salted duck egg must be cooked before it is eaten. The firm, bright orange yolk enhances the taste and appearance of moon cakes and is also used as an ingredient in other dishes.

Duck Gizzard, Dried 鴨腎乾

Dried duck gizzard is dark brown and hard. It is mostly used to flavor soups. When steamed on top of a pot of rice, it becomes chewy and tasty. This snack is enjoyed especially by children.

Fish, Salted 鹹魚

Many types of fish are salted. Some are then dried and others are preserved in oil. Salted fish is steamed, fried or added to other dishes to enhance their flavor. When cooked, salted fish tastes like canned anchovies. Chinese gourmets claim that the best salted fish comes from the city of Penang in Malaysia. Those from Tahiti and Venezuela are also considered to be very good.

Fish Air-Bladder, Dried 魚膠

Dried fish air-bladder is sold either unpuffed or puffed. The unpuffed air-bladder resembles a sheet of thick, hard semitransparent parchment and must be puffed before cooking. The puffed air-bladder looks like a piece of hard dry sponge. When cooked, the air-bladders are tasteless but have a nice texture and absorb sauces well. A banquet favorite is fish cake steamed on pieces of puffed fish air-bladder.

Five-Spice Powder 五香粉

This seasoning is a brownish mixture of five ground spices: star anise, peppercorn, cloves, cinnamon and fennel. The aromatic powder is used to season roasted meats and poultry.

Fungi, Dried

Many types of edible fungi are used as foods, such as the large "wood ears" 木耳, the small "*chuan* ears" 川耳 and the white "snow ears" 雪耳. Dried fungi are used in soups, vegetarian dishes and many other dishes as well.

Haisin Sauce 海鮮醬

This sweet sauce is made with soybean flour, red beans, ginger, garlic, chili, sugar and other spices. Haisin sauce is used as a condiment for shrimp, pork and poultry, and also for marinating meats.

Jellyfish, Dehydrated 海蜇皮

Dehydrated jellyfish is bland, crisp and crunchy. It is used with cold dishes or added to rice gruel 粥.

Jujube, Dried 紅棗

This datelike fruit, when dried, has a reddish

wrinkled skin. It imparts a sweet flavor to soups, stews and steamed dishes. The New Year pudding 年糕 is traditionally decorated with dried red jujubes to signify happiness. The red jujube, *hung tsao*, and "red early," *hung tsao* 紅早, are homonyms. "Red early" means "happiness early."

Lily Flower Buds, Dried 金菜

Dried lily flower buds are yellowish to golden brown in color and approximately four inches in length. They are used as dried vegetables.

Lily Bulb Scales, Dried 百合

The dried scales of the lily bulb are used as dried vegetables. They are added to soups and to the vegetarian dish *chai* 齋.

Long Beans 豆角

Long beans are yellowish green and resemble thin ropes about three-eighths of a inch in diameter. They are usually cut and stir fried.

Long beans

Lotus Root 蓮藕

The segmented, yellowish brown tubers of the water lily are rooted in muddy ponds. The tuber has many cavities running lengthwise and, when cut crosswise, shows many perforations. The fresh root is sweet and crunchy.

Lotus root

As a vegetable, it is stir fried or simmered in soups. When cooked and glazed with sugar, it is used as a sweetmeat.

Lotus Seeds 蓮子

Fresh lotus seeds are eaten raw or after being boiled in sugar. The dried seeds, which resemble nuts, are used in soups. They can also be made into sweetmeats. The candied lotus seeds symbolize many children because lotus seeds, *lien tzu*, and "successive children," *lien tzu* 連子, are homonyms.

Melon, Bitter 苦瓜

Bitter melon, which is also known as Balsam pear, resembles a warty cucumber. The bitter melon grown in the southern provinces of

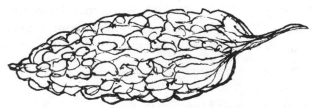

Bitter melon

China was introduced from the countries south of China. Bitter melon is stir fried or stuffed with meats and steamed. The flavor of bitter melon is an acquired taste but many Chinese savor it. Dried bitter melon is used as a medicine to lower fevers.

Melon, Fuzzy 毛瓜

This small greenish melon has a thin, delicate, fuzzy covering. It is cut into pieces and stir fried or added to soups.

Melon, Winter 冬瓜

This large, green, oblong-shaped melon has a thick, hard, frosty covering. It is often mistaken for a watermelon. The flesh of the melon is white and pulpy. The center is hollow and surrounded by seeds.

The melon is usually cut into pieces and added to soups. A banquet favorite is a soup made with chicken, pork, ham, mushrooms, lotus seeds, bamboo shoots, water chestnuts and crabmeat which is steamed in a topped winter melon.

Melon Seeds 瓜子

There are two types of watermelon seeds, the red and the black. The red watermelon seeds are smaller, have harder shells and are more expensive. These seeds are dried and roasted, and eaten as nuts during the New Year and at banquets.

Melon seeds symbolize many children because melon seeds, *kua tzu*, and "family children," *chia tzu* 家子, are close homonyms.

Mushrooms

Edible mushrooms, sold fresh, dried or canned, are used as ingredients in many dishes. Some of the edible mushrooms are the large black mushroom 冬菇, the straw mushroom 草菇 and a variety called *hsiang hsin* 香信, which is thinner and tougher than the black mushroom.

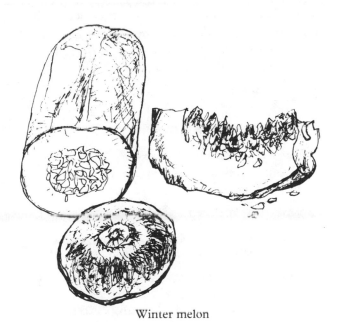

Winter melon

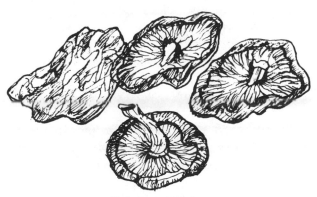

Dried mushrooms

Mustard Greens 芥菜

Mustard greens or mustard cabbage is a plant with green fan-shaped leaves. When partially cooked, it is crisp and has a slightly bitter taste. It is stir fried or added to soups.

Mustard greens pickled in brine is called salted cabbage 鹹菜 or sour cabbage 酸菜 and is usually stir fried.

Net Fat 網油

Net fat or caul fat is the lacy netlike fat from the abdomen of the pig. The delicate latticed fat is used to wrap fish cakes and minced oyster rolls.

Olive, Dried 欖豉

This is a partially dried olive which was cut in half, pitted and preserved in salt.

Dried preserved olives are steamed with oil, soy sauce and shredded ginger or with pork. They are also added to stuffings and to taro pudding 芋頭糕 to enhance their flavor.

Oysters, Dried 蠔豉

There are two types of dried oysters, the sun-dried raw oyster 生曬蠔豉 and the sun-dried cooked oyster 熟曬蠔豉. The sun-dried raw oyster is flat, firm, yellowish brown, skewered on a piece of bamboo and very expensive. It is delicious when steamed with oil, soy sauce and shredded ginger. The sun-dried cooked oyster is round, soft, reddish-brown, not skewered and much cheaper. This oyster was cooked and its essence extracted to make oyster sauce. The cooked oyster is used in many dishes. Minced and wrapped in net fat, it is used to make oyster rolls.

Oyster rolls made with dried cooked oysters are often served as the fourth course at banquets celebrating happy events because dried oysters, *hao shih*, sounds like "good four," *hao szu* 好四, and "good news," *hao shih* 好事.

Oysters, Fresh 生蠔

Fresh oysters are stir fried with ginger and scallions or lightly battered and deep fried.

Oyster Sauce 蠔油

Oyster sauce is made from the essence of oysters, salt, soy sauce and other seasonings. It is used as a flavoring agent or a dipping condiment to improve the taste of fried eggs, omelets, preserved duck eggs, chicken, roast pork and fried rice.

Plum Sauce 蘇梅醬

Plum sauce is also known as duck sauce because it is used as a condiment for roast duck. It is similarly used for roast pork. The chutney-like sauce is made from plum, apricot, vinegar, chili and sugar.

Prawns, Dried 大蝦乾

These prawns are butterflied with their shell and dried. They are also expensive and difficult to find. Dried prawns are delicious when steamed with or without stuffings.

Sausages 臘腸

Chinese sausages are usually made with pork or a mixture of pork and chopped duck liver. They are delicious when simply steamed or steamed with chicken or pork. Chopped sau-

Chinese sausages

sages added to minced meats 鬆 or to fried rice enhance their taste.

Sea Cucumber, Dried 海參

Sea cucumber is also known as beche-de-mer. This marine mollusk without a shell varies from four to twelve inches in length and resembles a cucumber. When dried, it is black and woodlike, and must be soaked and cleaned before cooking. It is considered a rare delicacy and is often served at banquets.

Dried sea cucumber

Seaweeds

There are many varieties of edible seaweed. Sea grass 海草 resembles grass runners. Sea ribbons 海帶 are flat and broad. Purple lavers 紫菜 are thin and paperlike.

Fresh seaweeds are parboiled or pickled and used as vegetables. However, most of the edible seaweeds are dried and used in soups.

Sesame Seed Oil 芝蔴油

This oil is extracted from toasted white sesame seeds. Sesame seed oil, a flavoring agent, is used very sparingly in soups, poultry and cold dishes.

Scallops, Dried 江瑤柱

The dried adductor muscle of this bivalved mollusk is brownish-yellow, disc-like and approximately one inch in diameter and a half inch thick. Children love to eat the uncooked dried scallop as a snack because it is chewy and has a slightly fishy taste. Dried scallops are used in soups or added to other dishes as a flavoring agent.

Shrimp, Dried 蝦米

There are two types of dried shrimp, the large and the small. The large dried shrimp 大蝦米 are about an inch in length and the smaller ones 蝦米仔 are about half an inch. The dried shrimp are used as flavoring agents.

Shrimp Sauce 蝦醬

Shrimp sauce is also called shrimp paste. This extremely pungent, salty, gray sauce is made from ground shrimp and is used as a flavoring agent. Its distinctive smell and flavor are almost identical to that of anchovy paste.

Snow Peas 雪豆

This flat green pea was probably introduced into China from Europe as early as the Han 漢 dynasty (206 B.C.–A.D. 220). When stir fried,

Snow peas

the peas with pods are sweet, tender and crispy.

Squash, Pleated 絲瓜

The pleated squash is known as the silk squash, Chinese okra, dish-rag squash or the victory squash. This sweet squash has a thin green covering and raised longitudinal ridges. It is used as a vegetable in stir fried dishes or added to soups. The dried ripened squash is very fibrous and is used as a dish rag to scour dishes and pans.

Pleated squash

Although the popular name for this squash is silk squash, *ssu kua,* some people, especially those who are superstitious and gamblers, renamed it victory squash, *sheng kua* 勝瓜, because silk, pronounced *ssu,* is similar to *shu* 輸, meaning "to lose."

Squid 魷魚

This slender marine mollusk with ten arms, of which two are longer than the others, is similar to a cuttlefish except that the squid is smaller and does not have a calcareous internal shell. The fresh squid is usually stir fried with vegetables or deep fried. Dried squid is stir fried, steamed or added to soups.

Tangerine Peel, Dried 菓皮

Dried tangerine peel is thin, brown and very pungent. It is used to flavor duck, meats and soups. A high-grade tangerine peel remains firm and retains its flavor even after a long period of boiling.

Conclusion

There is an old Chinese saying: "Drinking and eating are virtues" 飲和食德. It is hoped that those who savor Chinese food will also promote virtue.

CHAPTER 14

The Hakka

People living in the southern provinces of China, especially in the province of Kwangtung 廣東, made a distinction between the original inhabitants of the area, called Penti 本地, and visitors who came from elsewhere, called Ko Chia 客家 in the northern dialect and Hakka in the Cantonese dialect. Who were the Hakka and where did they come from? Why did they speak a different dialect and wear different costumes? Why was there so much animosity between the Penti and the Hakka? In this chapter we shall try to answer some of these questions.

The name Hakka dates back to a Tang 唐 dynasty census undertaken in the late eighth century. The term was used in this census to designate a specific group of clannish Chinese who kept to themselves, did not integrate with the local inhabitants and stood out as a different social group by virtue of their distinctive dialect and costume. It was not claimed, however, that the Hakka were one of the fifty or so minority races in China; rather, they were recognized as belonging to the Han 漢 race.

There are many theories regarding the origin and history of the Hakka. A widely accepted theory is that they originally lived in northern China and gradually moved south during times of political upheaval, oppression and persecution. Around the third century B.C., they lived principally in the provinces of Shantung 山東, Shansi 山西 and Anhui 安徽. During the oppressive and bloody reign of the first emperor of the Chin 秦 dynasty, around 221 B.C., the Hakka settled in the provinces of Honan 河南 and Kiangsi 江西. During the period of the Six Dynasties 六朝 (265-589), persecutions forced them to flee farther south and seek refuge in the mountainous regions of southeast Kiangsi bordering the province of Fukien 福建. During the Tang dynasty (618–906), most of the Hakka were compelled to move to the high mountains of Fukien. Others settled farther south in the mountainous areas separating the provinces of Kiangsi and Kwangtung. During the Ming 明 dynasty (1368–1644), disturbances and social unrest forced the Hakka who had lived in those areas for many centuries to move into the province of Kwangtung. In the Ching 清 dynasty (1644–1911), many Hakka settled in other southern provinces, including Kwangsi 廣西, Hunan 湖南 and Szechuan 四川. During the same period, they also moved to Taiwan 臺灣

and the island of Hainan 海南. Today the Hakka are scattered all over the world. They are found in Japan, Southeast Asia, the Philippines, Tahiti, North Borneo, Sri Lanka, Africa, Hawaii, California, Mexico, South America and Australia.

The Hakka dialect is closely akin to the dialect spoken in northern China. Some linguists claim that the Hakka dialect is actually closer to the ancient language spoken in northern China than it is to the present-day northern dialect because the modern northern dialect has changed as a result of the numerous invasions of nomadic tribes.

The rapidly disappearing Hakka costume is quite distinctive. A traditional Hakka woman typically wore a black kerchief over her head. Her hat, lacking a crown, was flat with a wide brim trimmed with a black cloth valance. Her jacket was quite long, reaching below the knees, and a plain black apron was usually

Hakka peasant woman's hat

worn with it. For formal and ceremonial occasions, a silk kerchief decorated with silver ornaments covered the head, and the plain black apron was exchanged for a black apron with a triangle of embroidery on the bib. A silver chain worn around the neck was hooked to a pair of ornaments sewn on the top of the bib. A woven ribbon was used to secure the apron at the waist.

The roles of men and women in Hakka families were not separated as strictly as they were in other Chinese families. The women did not adopt the custom of footbinding and were never sold as slaves or concubines. Polygamy was rare. In addition to their domestic duties, women helped to tend the fields, gathered wood and grass for fuel and fed the pigs.

Hakka cooking is similar to Cantonese cooking but is distinguished by its avoidance of the heavy use of garlic, spices or strong oils. A classic Hakka dish is salt-baked chicken, which is made by rubbing chicken with salt and baking it. It is simple but delicious. Hakka cooking is also noted for its *tou fu*, bell pepper and bitter melon stuffed with fish cake or minced meats, and puffed rice cakes 通米.

In matters of religion, the Hakka placed great emphasis on ancestral worship and on the use of *feng shui* 風水, a system of geomancy, to select favorable sites for homes, buildings, graves and roads. They primarily worshipped in temples dedicated to the Goddess of Mercy 觀音菩薩 and the God of War 關帝.

For the most part, the Hakka were poor peasants who worked hard and had to struggle to survive. As newcomers, they were forced to live in dry, barren hilly regions where the soil was less fertile. They were simple, brave, tough and aggressive. Some worked as barbers, itinerant blacksmiths and masons—vocations despised by the Penti. Yet a few, regardless of their lowly status, became wealthy, well educated and powerful government officials.

In the nineteenth century, the province of Kwangtung, an area of about 100,000 square miles, was divided into more than 70 administrative districts 縣. The Hakka, who made up about one-third of the population, were dispersed throughout the province in varying degrees of concentration. In some districts all the people were Hakka; in others their numbers were negligible.

Conflict between the Penti and Hakka, fueled by discrimination, prejudice and jealousy, led to feuds and even killings. Around 1850, the clashes began to escalate and became progressively worse in Kwangtung province. Between 1864 and 1866, the antagonism became so bitter and violent that the government was compelled to intervene. About eight thousand troops from Canton were dispatched to quell the terrible bloodshed in which more than 150,000 people had already perished. The Hakka were forced to surrender their arms. Some were given financial aid and relocated to the wastelands of Kwangsi, Hainan island and elsewhere. But the deep hostility between the Hakka and the Penti was very slow to dissipate.

Prominent Hakka

Hung Hsiu-Chuan and the Taiping Rebellion

One of the most notorious Hakka was Hung Hsiu-Chuan 洪秀全, who led a peasant rebellion that almost toppled the decadent Ching dynasty. He was born the youngest son of the Hung family on January 1, 1814, in Hua Hsien 花縣, a district about thirty miles north of the city of Canton. His moderately well-to-do father was a peasant who was able at great sacrifice to give him a few years of schooling. This gifted child was endowed with a remarkable aptitude for study and attended school from the age of seven to fifteen. Later he continued to study on his own and took the civil service examination in Kwangtung province several times without success. He then became a village school teacher.

In 1837, Hung came into possession of a pamphlet entitled "Good Advice to the World," put out by Christian missionaries, and glanced through it casually. The following year, after again failing the provincial civil service examination, he was afflicted with a psychiatric disorder and went into a coma that lasted for forty days. During that time, he experienced hallucinations, seeing visions of an old man accompanied by his two sons. After recovery, he re-read the missionary pamphlet carefully and concluded that the old man in his vision was God, the older son was Jesus Christ and he was the younger son, chosen to rid the world of idols and demons.

In 1847, Hung organized the poor peasants of the region into a religious cult. The members of the cult called themselves "God Worshippers." They worshipped a single God and rejected ancestral worship and the traditional Chinese gods. In 1850, Hung expanded the cult into a large peasant army called the "Heavenly Kingdom of Great Peace" 太平天國. With Hung Hsiu-Chuan as its leader, the army launched the Taiping Rebellion 太平伏 from the province of Kwangsi, adjoining Kwangtung, with the aim of overthrowing the Ching dynasty and instituting reforms. The rapidly expanding peasant army marched north. It took the city of Hankow 漢口 in 1852 and the city of Nanking 南京 in 1853.

From Nanking, which became their capital, they proceeded north toward the imperial capital of Peking, but did not reach their goal. They were driven back when they were about 130 kilometers from the capital. In 1864, Tseng Kuo-Fan 曾國藩, a learned Confucian scholar, and his able lieutenant Li Hung-Chang 李鴻章 organized a volunteer army in Hunan 湖南 province. This army together with the imperial forces fought the rebels.

Some of the Western missionaries were initially pleased with the success of the rebels. They thought that the rebels' belief in a single God and his son, Jesus Christ, could pave the way for the ultimate conversion of China to Christianity. However, the governments of the United States and England realized that if the fanatical rebels were successful in overthrowing the Ching dynasty, they could well eliminate the preferential advantages in trade which the Western powers had gained in China. An American adventurer, Frederick Townsend Ward from Salem, Massachusetts, was permitted to lead the imperial army against the rebels. After he was killed in battle, a British soldier, Major Charles George Gordon, also known as "Chinese Gordon," replaced him.

The combined forces defeated the rebels when Nanking fell in the summer of 1864. Hung Hsiu-Chuan, together with many of his officers and peasant soldiers, committed suicide several weeks before the final defeat.

The Taiping Rebellion was the greatest civil war in the history of mankind. No war had caused such destruction and loss of life until the great wars of the present century. Five provinces and more than six hundred walled cities were destroyed and left in shambles. Although there were no accurate statistics of the number of people killed, the most conservative estimate is that over twenty million people perished.

Charles J. Soong

A well-known Hakka family that played a prominent role in modern Chinese history was the family of Charles J. Soong 宋嘉樹. He and his children were powerful leaders of Republican China following the overthrow of the Ching dynasty in 1911.

The reports on the early life of Charles Soong are fragmentary and filled with discrepancies. Possibly the most authentic account is that his Hakka ancestors first settled as refugees on Hainan island following the Manchu conquest of China in 1644. His extended family were merchants who sailed their Hainan junks laden with goods to Macao 澳門, Swatow 汕頭 and Amoy 廈門, cities along the southern coast of China. When the winds were favorable, they traded as far as Annam 安南, Siam 暹羅, Malaya 馬來亞 and Java 爪哇, countries along the Pacific rim south of China.

Charles Soong was born in 1866 on Hainan island. His original surname was Han 韓 and his given name was Chia-Shu 嘉樹. At an early age, he was an indentured servant of a relative on Hainan. As a child, he made short trips on the junks with his uncles and brothers.

In 1878, at age twelve, he was taken to Boston by an "adopted uncle" who was a distant relative. There he worked in a tea and silk shop. At that time, there were very few Chinese in Boston. They were mainly students from wealthy families who had been sent abroad to acquire a modern Western education. These students often visited the shop where Chia-

Shu worked to drink tea, chat and discuss ways of helping China modernize. They advised Chia-Shu to attend school and prepare himself for a profession.

Chia-Shu tried several times to obtain a permit to enter school. Each time he was rebuffed. In 1879, after still another refusal, he boarded a cutter named the *Albert Gallatin* as a stowaway. This vessel was a Revenue Service ship of the U.S. Treasury Department. When the ship was in blue water and far from land, Chia-Shu was discovered and brought before Captain Eric Gabrielson. When asked his name, he replied that it was Chia-Shu. The captain thought he said Charles Sun and recorded this name in the ship's muster roll. In addition, Chia-Shu claimed that he was sixteen, the legal age for enlistment. He later changed his surname Sun to Soon because it sounded that way to him.

A special bond developed between Charles Soon and Captain Gabrielson. Charles was employed as a cabin boy and, through Gabrielson's efforts, was converted to Christianity. In 1880, he was baptized in a Southern Methodist church in Wilmington, North Carolina. At his baptism, he chose the name Charles Jones Soon.

The congregation was impressed with the new convert. They arranged for him to be educated and planned to make him a Christian missionary to serve his own people in China. He was enrolled as a special student at Trinity College. This college later became Duke University. He continued his education at the School of Religion of Vanderbilt University in Nashville, Tennessee.

In 1886, after Charles J. Soon was rushed through an accelerated program at Vanderbilt, Bishop Holland N. McTyerie, the chancellor at Vanderbilt, who was also in charge of the Southern Methodist Mission in China, sent Charles Soon to Shanghai. There Charles again changed his surname, refining Soon to Soong. In 1887, in spite of his low pay as a preacher, he managed to marry a young lady who came from one of China's oldest and most illustrious Chinese Christian families.

In 1890, he resigned from the mission and founded the Sino-American Press. He became wealthy by printing Bibles and reprinting Western books on history, science and technology. He used some of his wealth to help finance the planning of Dr. Sun Yat-sen's 孫逸仙 revolution.

Of his six children—three daughters and three sons—five supported Chiang Kai-Shek 蔣介石 and the Kuomingtang 國民黨 and one sided with Mao Tse-Tung 毛澤東 and the Communists in China's civil war. Those who supported Chiang Kai-Shek became extremely powerful and wealthy.

Charles Soong's daughters were Soong Ai-Ling 宋藹齡, who married H. H. Kung 孔祥熙, the finance minister of the Kuomingtang and the principal banker in China; Soong Ching-Ling 宋慶齡, a dedicated revolutionary who married Dr. Sun Yat-sen and remained in the People's Republic of China after 1949; and Soong May-Ling 宋美齡, who married Chiang Kai-Shek and became the powerful First Lady of China.

Charles Soong's sons were T. V. Soong 宋子文, who at various times served as Chiang Kai-Shek's economics minister, finance minister and premier; T. L. Soong 宋子良, a financier who was in charge of U.S. Lend-Lease to China during World War II; and T.

A. Soong 宋子安, also a financier, who was chairman of the board of the Bank of Canton in San Francisco.

Teng Hsiao-Ping and Yeh Chien-Ying

Two important Hakka who rose to the highest positions in the People's Republic of China are Teng Hsiao-Ping 鄧小平 and Yeh Chien-Ying 葉劍英. Teng Hsiao-Ping was born in 1904. His birthplace was about one hundred kilometers from Chungking 重慶 in Szechuan province. He was the second child of the second wife of a Hakka landlord who had emigrated from Kwangtung 廣東 province. He studied in France and Russia, joined the Chinese Communist Party in 1925 and gradually ascended the Communist hierarchy. He was a resilient leader who was twice publicly disgraced and purged from office. But each time, he rebounded and resumed positions of power.

In 1966, during the disastrous Cultural Revolution, Teng Hsiao-Ping was attacked by Red Guards. He was forced to parade down the streets wearing a dunce cap and was stripped of all his powers. He was rehabilitated and returned to power in October 1973 when Premier Chou En-Lai 周恩來 made him Vice-Premier of the State Council, the highest organ of the national government.

On April 5, 1976, during the Clear and Bright 清明 festival honoring the departed revolutionary heroes of modern China, Teng delivered a speech praising the late Premier Chou En-Lai. Rioting followed. Mao Tse-Tung's wife, Chiang Ching 江青, and her three cohorts in the "Gang of Four" 四人幫 accused Teng of instigating the trouble. Two days later he was again publicly disgraced and stripped of his powers.

Mao-Tse Tung died on September 9, 1976. A month later, on October 6, the "Gang of Four" was arrested and jailed. Teng Hsiao-Ping returned to office and subsequently became the foremost leader of the People's Republic of China. He is credited with initiating the reform movement and the "Open Door" policy, two key ingredients in China's drive toward modernization in the last decades of the twentieth century.

Marshal Yeh Chien-Ying was a native of Kwangtung province. Although he was a Hakka, he also spoke fluent Cantonese. He was a brilliant military officer who fought the Japanese and later the troops of Chiang Kai-Shek. After the establishment of the People's Republic of China on October 1, 1949, he became the nation's highest military officer and a member of the powerful Politburo of the Communist Party.

CHAPTER 15

Civil Service Examinations

The concept of using civil service examinations to select qualified people to administer the government originated in China about two thousand years ago. From 163 B.C., public written examinations stressing a knowledge of ethics were given sporadically. It was not until A.D. 706, in the Tang 唐 dynasty, that these public examinations came into general use as a basis for appointments to official positions. After that, the civil service examination system was improved and strengthened through subsequent dynasties. Its use continued almost to the end of the Ching 清 dynasty in the early part of this century.

From 1370, in the Ming 明 dynasty, through the greater part of the Ching dynasty (1644–1911), civil service examinations were held on the district, provincial and national levels. These examinations were progressively more elaborate and gruelling, stressing literary knowledge of the Confucian and other ancient classics. They ignored scientific and technical knowledge. Successful candidates, after passing each examination level, were granted degrees and conferred certain privileges and honors.

The initial written examination was held every two years in all administrative districts 縣 of a province. An average of two thousand candidates took the examination in each district. A candidate was confined in a small cubicle for a day and a night. The individual had to compose two essays and a poem. These compositions had to be written in the old literary style and were judged on their calligraphy and understanding of the classics. Only about twenty of the candidates, or 1 percent, passed the qualifying examination. Those who passed were granted the degree of Budding Genius 秀才.

A Budding Genius was respected by friends and neighbors, held in high regard as a scholar and welcomed among the local gentry. His opinion was often sought where learning was required. He was exempt from taxes and from corporal punishment imposed by the district magistrates. He was entitled to adorn his cap with the lowest-grade gold button. Occasionally, a Budding Genius was appointed to serve as a minor district official. More importantly, he was permitted to become a candidate for the provincial examination.

The provincial examination was held triennially, usually in early autumn, at the provin-

Examination hall cubicles

cial capital. In every provincial capital, thousands of cubicles were constructed for this examination. The second examination was much more formidable and consisted of three sessions. Each session lasted three days. The supervisors who conducted the examination were appointed by the emperor. The night be-

fore the examination, amid great pomp and ceremony, including a prayer and the exploding of firecrackers, the candidates were led to their cells and sealed in for the entire duration. A candidate was required to compose thirteen essays written in literary style on topics selected from the classics and a poem containing eight couplets. The ordeal was so severe that it was not unheard of for a candidate to die in his small enclosed cell from the extreme physical and mental strain of the examination. Depending on the size of the province, candidates for the provincial examination numbered from three thousand to seventeen thousand. About 1 percent of these candidates passed and were granted the degree of Elevated Man 舉人.

The Elevated Men were honored at a banquet. Each was given a robe and an official cap decorated with a higher-grade gold button. Each was also given twenty taels of silver, provided by the provincial treasury, to erect flag poles over the family gate and a wooden table above the door informing people that the family had produced an Elevated Man.

Although an Elevated Man was held in higher esteem than a Budding Genius, he was still not entitled to hold office. Generally, a scholar was eligible to hold office only after he had passed the national examination. This examination was held triennially, in the spring following the provincial examinations, at the imperial palace in Peking. Only Elevated Men were permitted to take this examination. Candidates from all over the country converged at the nation's capital. A candidate's expenses during the examination period were subsidized by the provincial treasury.

This examination consisted of only one session lasting three days. Candidates were judged on their calligraphy and on the essays and poems they wrote dealing with current political problems such as irrigation, colonization, water conservation and education. The style of composition again had to conform to the literary style of the old classics. Originality was frowned upon.

About 1 percent of the candidates passed the national examination. Those who passed were awarded the degree of Achieved Scholar 進士. The new Achieved Scholars took another examination whose results were used in ranking them.

The emperor himself honored the new Achieved Scholars at a banquet. They dined with high officials and were showered with congratulations. Signboards and posters in red and yellow proclaimed their success. The most successful of all were the top three scholars, who were singled out to receive special honors. The highest on the list was given the title "Model Scholar of the Land" 狀元. The second received the title "Proclamation Eye" 榜眼. The third was bestowed the title "Visitation Flower" 探花.

The "Model Scholar of the Land" was held in the highest public esteem. He was eligible to marry a princess. The lowest position available to him was that of a viceroy and he had good reason to believe that he would eventually occupy the highest administrative office in the empire.

Approximately one-third of the Achieved Scholars qualified for admission to the Hanlin Academy 翰林院, the Forest of Pencils. They were considered the poets and historians of the empire and could be appointed as provincial chancellors and examiners. Other Achieved Scholars were eligible to hold office in the future. Lots were drawn to fill vacant posts. The fortunate ones often started their official careers as district magistrates.

The civil service examination system allowed everyone, regardless of social status and rank, to qualify for higher office by virtue of his ability, however narrowly defined that ability might be. Successful candidates from the humblest families were able to rise in public esteem, status, power and wealth. Since the examinations were public, they were conducted properly and fairly for the most part. Above all, they helped to stress the importance of education and promoted national unity.

Nevertheless, the Chinese civil service examination system had many faults. Even though people from poor families could in theory take the examinations, actually only the wealthy could afford the many years required to prepare for the examinations. Moreover, the heavy stress on literary knowledge as the primary goal of education discouraged vocational training and study in other fields such as the social and natural sciences. The exclusive focus on the ancient classics perpetuated the status quo and stifled independent thinking. Countless hours were spent on rote memory. Finally, it can be doubted whether beautiful calligraphy and a good literary style were sufficient criteria for determining whether an individual would be able to administer efficiently the various functions of a complex government.

In 1905 the antiquated civil service examination system was judged to be obsolete and abolished.

Nevertheless, although ultimately discarded as a system that had outlived its usefulness, the Chinese civil service examinations did influence the development of similar examinations in the West, where the concept of basing appointments on merit rather than patronage came as a startling new idea. As early as the sixteenth century, Jesuit missionaries in China wrote favorably about the Chinese system, stimulating the development of the new European academies of learning. These progressive currents led France to adopt a system of civil service examinations in 1791. Germany did the same around 1800, and India followed suit in 1855. England then applied the Indian system for all home services in 1870. In the United States, civil service examinations were initiated in 1883 when Congress passed the Pendleton Bill, which became the first Civil Service Act.

CHAPTER 16

Education in China

Although schooling varied considerably in different parts of old China, most of the people had little or no formal education. One reason for this lack is that practical training was never a concern of the schools. Knowledge of farming was transmitted orally from a peasant to his sons. Guilds conducted their own vocational training through a system of apprenticeship. A daughter was taught how to perform household duties by her mother or grandmother so that she could obediently serve her future husband and parents-in-law. The net result, according to some estimates, is that 80 percent of the people were unable to read or write.

The goals of a formal education in old China were limited to preparing a student for only two professions—either as a Buddhist priest or as a government official. The goal of preparing for the priesthood had very little influence on the educational system. Consequently, the primary objective of formal education was to prepare a student to pass the civil service examinations. The school's curriculum consisted of studying and memorizing the ancient classics, refining one's calligraphy and practice in composing letters, essays and poems in the old literary style.

Generally, the schools were poorly or-ganized. The teachers were usually individuals who had passed the civil service examination on either the district or provincial level. These teachers, although highly regarded, had not been trained as teachers and were poorly paid for their services. There were other alternatives. Wealthy families could and did employ private tutors for their children. Scholars occasionally taught their own sons and grandsons. Several families could combine their resources and employ a teacher who held classes in the clan hall, temple hall or a rented room.

Whatever the structure, discipline in the school was strict. Students read aloud after the teacher. They were required first of all to memorize the classics; understanding them was a secondary goal. Students were tested by having to recite a text verbatim to the teacher without referring to the book. Discussion of the text only took place after it had been memorized.

In calligraphy, students were first taught how to execute the basic strokes of the characters with a brush pen. After that, they learned to write simple characters by means of tracing and copying. Later they learned to write the characters in the different styles that displayed the various qualities of beauty and strength.

A student learned to compose letters, essays and poems in the old literary style because the civil service examinations were based on that style. Writing in the vernacular was considered to be crude, vulgar and lacking in culture. If a student's composition lacked the proper polish, it would be corrected by the teacher until it conformed to the right style. As a result, the meanings of phrases, sentences and entire paragraphs were often vague and imprecise.

Most students dropped out after one or two years of formal schooling. Only a few students—those who possessed special ability or those whose families could afford many years of formal education—were adequately prepared to take the civil service examinations.

From about the end of the nineteenth century, progressive Chinese intellectuals realized that their country was backward and in need of sweeping reforms so that it could enter the modern world. A wide range of reforms was proposed and discussed, encompassing the old forms of ethics and customs, the educational system, the fields of literature, history, philosophy, religion and economics, and the existing social and political institutions. The new ideas came from many sources, including missionaries and other foreigners living in China. Ideas for reform were also brought back by Chinese students who had studied abroad in Japan, the United States and Europe.

The prospect for reform was greatly enhanced by the May Fourth Movement, the intellectual revolution of modern China. It covered a period of four years from 1917 to 1921, centering on the May Fourth Incident of 1919. The first phase, prior to the incident, was one of preparation. The second phase, following the incident, was one of implementation.

During the first phase of the May Fourth Movement, progressive intellectuals instilled new and revolutionary concepts in the students of China. The May Fourth Incident succeeded in igniting a spirit of nationalism and unifying the country around certain ideas. It made possible the subsequent phase, which was to initiate the actual reforms. These reforms would have profound consequences, ultimately transforming the face of China.

The May Fourth Incident arose as a reaction to the inequitable treaties signed by the Allied powers at the Versailles Peace Conference in April 1919. The key provision was that all the leases and rights in the province of Shantung 山東 which China had previously granted to Germany would henceforth be transferred to Japan rather than revert to China, one of the Allied powers. When news of this provision reached China, a huge demonstration was held in Peking on May 4, 1919, to protest the treaty. This protest spread rapidly throughout the country. All segments of the population, including students, intellectuals, merchants, tradesmen and peasants, were caught up in a tidal wave of sentiment.

The reforms that were meant to follow, however, were slow in coming because of numerous obstacles and difficulties. The country was poor. A large percentage of the people were illiterate. Conservatives opposed modernization for fear that China would lose her identity. Many felt it was better to maintain the status quo. There were also frequent disruptions in the campaign for reform because of growing political unrest, changes of leadership in the various camps and the outbreak of civil war.

Credit for introducing a new educational system to China must be given to the Christian missionaries, especially those from English and American Protestant churches. Although the

Roman Catholics in China started schools for children, these schools were primarily intent on training Chinese men for the Catholic priesthood. The Protestants, on the other hand, set up primary schools for children of the poorer classes. They later expanded these institutions and opened boarding schools to educate children of both sexes. At that time, schools for girls were considered most unusual in China.

The mission schools prepared students to meet the demands of modern society and the real world. Classes were conducted in English, and the curriculum included courses in classical Chinese literature, philosophy, mathematics, geography, history, social and political science, the natural sciences and of course Christian scripture. Since there were very few Chinese texts on modern subjects, these schools had the effect of opening up a vast storehouse of knowledge to the Chinese.

The development of secondary schools and universities followed. Some of the universities conferred degrees. Some were affiliated with universities abroad, so that academic work completed by students in China would be recognized and qualify the students for graduate studies abroad.

Following the Boxer Rebellion in 1900, the United States had remitted $22.4 million of the Boxer Rebellion Indemnity Fund for the purpose of upgrading China's educational system and to provide scholarships for deserving students to study in America. In 1915, there were over 1,500 Chinese students studying in American colleges and universities.

One of these students was Hu Shih 胡適, who received a B.A. degree from Cornell University in 1915. Continuing his studies in philosophy, he obtained a Ph.D. from Columbia University in 1917. As a "returned student," Hu Shih became a professor in philosophy at Peking University in 1917 and remained on that faculty until 1927. Later he went on to hold a series of distinguished posts, including chairman of the Department of English Literature, dean of the School of Letters, ambassador to the United States and chancellor of Peking University.

Hu Shih and others stressed the importance of writing in the vernacular 白話 rather than the difficult and vague literary style of the classics. He concluded that in matters of self-expression eight principles were to be recommended:

1. Avoid the use of classical allusions.
2. Discard stale, time-worn literary phrases.
3. Discard the parallel construction of sentences.
4. Do not avoid using vernacular words or speech.
5. Follow literary grammar.
6. Do not write that you are sick or sad when you do not feel sick or sad.
7. Do not imitate the writings of the ancients; what one writes should reflect one's own personality.
8. What one writes should have real meaning and substance.

In 1918 James Y. C. Yen 晏陽初, another "returned student" who had studied in the United States under the sponsorship of the Young Men's Christian Association (YMCA), inaugurated the Mass Education Movement. To teach adult illiterates, he compiled a list of about 1,300 Chinese characters representing the words most commonly used in vernacular speech and literature. He called this list the "Thousand

Character Lessons" 千字課 and demonstrated that those characters could be learned in a comparatively short period of time, thus enabling adults to read and write in a simple but effective manner. In addition, he believed that the knowledge of those characters would stimulate the students to learn more characters.

In the early 1920s, educators from the United States surveyed the Chinese educational system. Professor (later president) Ernest De-Witt Burton from the University of Chicago evaluated the Protestant schools in China. Dr. Paul Monroe from Columbia University served as an advisor to the Chinese Ministry of Education. The two educators proposed methods of upgrading the school system and made recommendations concerning the course of future development.

The number of schools and students at all levels increased tremendously under the Republic of China. A comparison of figures reported in 1912, the first year of the Republic, and figures reported 25 years later in 1937 showed amazing gains. In 1912 there were 83,319 elementary schools with an enrollment of nearly 2.8 million students. In 1937 there were 259,000 elementary schools with nearly 11.7 million students. During the same period, the number of secondary or middle schools increased from 373 schools with 52,000 students to some 3,000 secondary schools (including normal and vocational schools) with over 500,000 students. Moreover, in 1912 there were only 4 schools that had college or university standards, with a total enrollment of 481 students, whereas in 1937 there were 108 colleges and universities with 42,900 students.

Following the advent of the People's Republic of China in 1949, further gains in educa-tion have been made. According to the 1980 *World Almanac*, the literacy rate in China in 1975 was an amazing 95 percent. This spectacular accomplishment means that in this century the illiteracy rate in China has dropped from 80 percent to a mere 5 percent.

The spread of literacy in the People's Republic has been aided by the first successful effort to simplify complicated Chinese characters by reducing the number of strokes needed to write them. By government decree, thousands of complicated characters were simplified. The same scheme was subsequently adopted by the Japanese. A few examples of the simplified characters follow:

醫 "to heal" is now 医
國 "country" is now 国
學 "to learn" is now 学
廣 "broad" is now 广
華 "beauty" or "splendor" is now 华

Many methods of anglicizing Chinese words have been invented. The Wade-Giles system used in older textbooks and dictionaries was developed in the late nineteenth century. The Yale system was developed around 1940 and has been used mainly in teaching Chinese in the United States. The most recent is the *pinyin* 拼音 system, a further development of the Yale system. Many linguists agree that the *pinyin* system provides the simplest and most accurate transcription of Chinese sounds.

Pinyin is pronounced phonetically with a few exceptions. The exceptions are mainly the following:

Consonants
c is pronounced like the ts in tsetse fly.

q is pronounced like the ch in chin.
x is pronounced like the sh in sheen.
zh is pronounced like the j in jump.

Vowels
e is pronounced like the e in talent.
i before ng is pronounced like the u in rung.
o is pronounced like the aw in jaw.
ou is pronounced like the o in go.

In 1958 the People's Republic of China adopted *pinyin* as the official system for anglicizing Chinese words. In 1976 *pinyin* spellings became standard for placenames and other names. Some examples follow:

Places
Fukien to Fujian 福建
Kwangsi to Guangxi 廣西
Kwangtung to Guangdong 廣東
Kweilin to Guilin 桂林
Macao to Aoman 澳門

Peking to Beijing 北京
Sian to Xian 西安
Tientsin to Tianjin 天津
Tsingtao to Qingdao 青島

Names
Chin to Qin 秦
Chou En-Lai to Zhou Enlai 周恩來
Mao Tse-Tung to Mao Zedong 毛澤東
Teng Hsiao-Ping to Deng Xiaoping 鄧小平
Tsao Tsao to Cao Cao 曹操

Educational reforms in China have come a long way since the first halting attempts in the early part of this century, but they are far from over. The Chinese Ministry of Education of the People's Republic of China is continuing to improve methods of learning. Scholars are pressing forward with their experiments and further developments will undoubtedly be forthcoming.

CHAPTER 17

Couplets and Toasts

Scholars composed couplets to express their good wishes on various occasions. These couplets were written and posted or delivered as toasts. The number of couplets that a learned person could write was limited only by his literary talent. The couplets included here are traditional and have been translated freely.

Spring Couplets

Spring couplets 春聯, also known as New Year couplets, were written and posted at the home or at the place of business. This tradition began in the Ming 明 dynasty, at the beginning of the fifteenth century. Spring couplets expressed wishes for happiness, good health, longevity, wealth, prosperity, the gift of many sons, good harvests, tranquility and other blessings for the New Year.

Usually the four characters of each couplet were written lengthwise, from top to bottom, with gold ink on a sheet of red rectangular paper. The sheet of paper was approximately $9\frac{1}{2}$ by $4\frac{1}{2}$ inches or $11\frac{1}{2}$ by 5 inches, and was either plain red or red decorated with multicolored designs around the borders.

The couplets were posted in pairs, on both sides of the doors or on the walls of the halls before the New Year. These were left posted for an entire year and then replaced with new ones. The old couplets had to be disposed of properly by burning, for depositing the old couplets in a trashcan meant throwing away the blessings and good wishes.

A scholar skilled in calligraphy, one who was able to use the brush pen to write the characters with strength and elegance, often supplemented his income before the New Year by writing and selling spring couplets. These couplets could be purchased directly from the writer or through shops and organizations.

The use of spring couplets was not limited to the New Year festivities. Appropriate ones could be used on other occasions as well.

Some traditional New Year couplets follow:

1. Wishing you a happy New Year.
   恭賀新禧
2. Wishing you a prosperous New Year.
   恭喜發財
3. May you be blessed with good fortune during the New Year.
   新春大吉

4. May you enjoy happiness during the New Year.
新春納福

5. May you enjoy happiness when greeting the New Year.
迎春接福

6. May you enjoy continued good health.
出入平安

7. May you enjoy good health throughout the four seasons.
四季平安

8. Good health to everyone.
老少平安

9. Long life and prosperity.
長命富貴

10. Happiness, long life, good health and tranquility.
福壽康寧

11. Happiness, prosperity, long life and marital bliss.
福祿壽囍

12. May the five blessings approach your door.
五福臨門
The five blessings are old age, prosperity, good health, love of virtue and a natural death.

13. May your vitality be vigorous like that of the dragon and the horse.
龍馬精神

14. May your vitality be lively and strong.
精神爽利

15. May you succeed and prosper in all your endeavors.
萬事順利

16. May all your wishes come true.
萬事勝意

17. May you experience smooth sailing in all your endeavors.
一帆風順

18. Good luck in all your wishes.
如意吉祥

19. May you fulfill all your heart's desires.
得心應手

20. May you follow your heart's desire (without transgression).
從心所欲

21. May you succeed in the development of your great plans.
大展鴻圖

22. May you ascend and advance steadily step by step.
步步高陞

23. May you soar like the Peng bird for thousands of miles.
鵬程萬里
The Peng is a mythical bird of enormous size, capable of flying great distances and soaring to great heights.

24. May your descendants and wealth both flourish.
丁財兩旺

25. May you prosper throughout the year.
週年旺相

26. May your halls be filled with yellow gold.
黃金滿堂

27. May your halls be filled with treasures of gold and jade.
金玉滿堂

28. May your home be filled with gold and good fortune.
金吉滿堂

29. May you be blessed with good luck in the future.
鴻運當頭

30. May the Three Stars—the Star of Happiness, the Star of Wealth and the Star of Longevity—shine upon you.
三星拱照

31. May you enjoy good fortune and great profits.
    大吉大利
32. May you become prosperous when the flowers bloom.
    花開富貴
33. May you receive unexpected wealth.
    橫財就手
34. May your road to riches be free and clear.
    利路亨通
35. May your source of wealth increase and make broad advances.
    財源廣進
36. May your investment reap great profits.
    一本萬利
37. Prosperity and good business.
    發財好市
38. Harmony and prosperity.
    和氣生財
39. May your business continue to prosper.
    生意興隆
40. May your business continue to expand.
    基業宏開

Wedding Couplets

1. May the bride and groom be blessed with happiness and prosperity.
   鴛鴦福祿
   Yuan Yang 鴛鴦, a pair of mandarin ducks, allude to the bride and groom.
2. May you continue to have worthy sons.
   連生貴子
3. May your home be filled with sons and grandsons.
   子孫滿堂
4. May you be blessed with one hundred sons and one thousand grandsons.
   百子千孫

5. May you live in harmony for one hundred years.
   百年好合
6. May you grow old together for one hundred years.
   百年偕老
7. May you grow old together gracefully.
   白頭偕老
8. May you grow old together in harmony.
   同諧白髮
9. May you continue to prosper for five generations.
   五世其昌
10. May you treat each other with mutual respect.
    相敬如賓
11. This marriage was made in Heaven.
    天作之合
12. This marriage was arranged in Heaven.
    姻緣天定
13. The pairing of this happy couple was completed in Heaven.
    佳偶天成
14. This is a union of a precious pearl and an elegant jade.
    珠聯璧合
15. May this be a close and happy marriage.
    蒂結良緣

Birthday Couplets

1. Congratulations and happy birthday.
   恭祝華誕
2. May your felicity be as expansive as the Eastern Ocean
   (And) your longevity be as everlasting as the Southern Mountain.
   福如東海
   壽比南山

3. May your longevity be boundless.
   萬壽無疆
4. May the sacred peach bestow upon you long life.
   仙桃祝壽
5. Wealth and great honors.
   富貴榮華
6. Bountiful blessings and long life.
   多福多壽
   or
   長福長壽
7. May you have worthy grandsons and dutiful sons.
   孫賢子孝
8. May you be robust and majestic like the pine and the cypress.
   松柏之茂

9. May this day be repeated year after year.
   年年有今日
   or
   歲歲有今朝

Funeral Couplets

1. May the soul return to the kingdom of Heaven.
   魂歸天國
2. May the sacred crane return to the West.
   仙鶴歸西
3. May the soul experience eternal bliss in the West.
   西方極樂

BIBLIOGRAPHY

Austin, Robert, Dana Levy, and Veda Koichiro. *Bamboo*. Tokyo: Weatherhill, 1970.

Ball, J. Dyer. *Things Chinese*. Shanghai: Kelly and Walsh, 1892.

Bodde, Derk. *Annual Customs and Festivals in Peking*. Shanghai: North-China Daily News, 1936. Reprint. Hong Kong: Hong Kong University Press, 1965.

Bredon, Juliet, and Igo Mitrophanow. *The Moon Year*. Shanghai: Kelly and Walsh, 1927. Reprint. New York: Paragon, 1966.

Brewitt-Taylor, C. H. *Romance of the Three Kingdoms*. Shanghai: Kelly and Walsh, 1925. Reprint. Tokyo: Charles E. Tuttle, 1959.

Buchanan, Keith, Charles P. Fitzgerald, and Colin A. Ronan. *China: The Land and the People*. New York: Crown, 1980.

Burkhardt, V. R. *Chinese Creeds and Customs*. 3 vols. Hong Kong: South China Morning Post, 1958.

Callis, Helmut G. *China—Confucian and Communist*. New York: Henry Holt, 1973.

Capon, Edmund, and William MacQuitty. *Prince of Jade*. New York: Dutton, 1973.

Carter, Michael. *Crafts of China*. New York: Doubleday, 1977.

Chang, K. C. *Food in Chinese Culture*. New Haven, Conn: Yale University Press, 1977.

Chang, Wonona W., Irving Chang, Helene Kutscher, and Austin H. Kutscher. *Encyclopedia of Chinese Food and Cooking*. New York: Crown, 1970.

Char, Tin-Yuke. *The Bamboo Path*. Honolulu: Hawaii Chinese History Center, 1977.

China Science and Technology Palace Preparatory Committee and The Ontario Science Center. *China—7,000 Years of Discovery*. Ontario: Ontario Science Center, 1982.

Chow, Tse-Tung. *The May Fourth Movement*. Stanford: Stanford University Press, 1967.

Christie, Anthony. *Chinese Mythology*. London: Hamlyn, 1968.

Chu, Arthur, and Grace Chu. *Collector's Book of Jade*. New York: Crown, 1978.

Clayre, Alasdair. *The Heart of the Dragon*. Boston: Houghton Mifflin, 1985.

Cohen, Joan Lebold, and Jerome Allan. *China Today and Her Ancient Treasures*. New York: Abrams, 1980.

Coye, Molly J., and Jon Livingston. *China—Yesterday and Today*. New York: Bantam, 1979.

Dusfrene, C. Richard. "Inter-cultural Funeral Practices in Hawaii." Doctoral thesis. San Francisco Theological Seminary, 1981.

Du Halde, P. J. B. *A Description of the Empire of China*. Translated by Edward Cave. 2 vols. London: T. Gardner, 1738.

Eberhard, Wolfram. *Chinese Festivals*. London: Abelard-Schuman, 1958.

Goodrich, Anne S. *Chinese Hells*. St. Augustin: Monumenta Serica, 1981.

Goodrich, L. Carrington. *Short History of the Chinese People*. New York: Harper, 1951.

Gosier, J. B. *The World of Ancient China*. Geneva: Minerva, 1972.

Gray, J. H. *China: A History of Laws, Manners and Customs of the People*. 2 vols. London: Macmillan, 1878. Reprint. Shannon, Ireland: Irish University Press, 1972.

Greene, Felix. *Peking*. New York: Mayflower Books, 1978.

Gump, Richard. *Jade: Stone of Heaven*. New York: Doubleday, 1962.

Herold, A. F. *The Life of Buddha*. Tokyo: Charles E. Tuttle, 1952.

Howell, F. Clark. *Early Man*. New York: Time-Life Book Division, Nature Library, 1965.

Hsu, Francis L. K. *Under the Ancestors' Shadow*. London: Routledge and Kegan Paul, 1949.

Huang, Su Hei. *Chinese Snacks*. Taipei: Wei-Chuan, 1976.

Huard, Pierre, and Ming Wong. *Chinese Medicine*. World University Library. New York: McGraw Hill, 1968.

Hyde, Nina. "Queen of Textiles." *National Geographic* 165, no. 1 (January 1984).

Keys, John D. *Chinese Herbs*. Tokyo: Charles E. Tuttle, 1976.

Latourette, Kenneth S. *The Chinese: Their History and Culture*. New York: Macmillan, 1951.

Lee, H. T. *The Story of Chinese Culture*. Taiwan: 1964.

Lee, James Zee-Min. *Chinese Potpourri*. Hong Kong: Oriental Publisher, 1950.

Levy, Howard S. *Chinese Footbinding*. New York: Walter Rawls, 1966.

McNair, Harley F. *China*. Berkeley and Los Angeles: University of California Press, 1946.

Maitland, Derek. *5000 Years of Tea*. New York: Gallery Books, 1982.

Miller, Gloria B. *A Thousand Recipe Chinese Cookbook*. New York: Grosset and Dunlap, 1962.

Moore, Ruth. *Evolution*. New York: Time-Life Book Division, Nature Library, 1962.

Nagel's Encyclopedia-Guide. *China*. Geneva: Nagel Publishers, 1973.

Needham, Joseph. *Clerks and Craftsmen in China and the West*. Cambridge: Cambridge University Press, 1970.

Read, Bernard E. "Chinese Materia Medica—Animal Drugs." *Peking Natural History Bulletin*, vol. 5, pt. 4, pp. 37–80; vol. 6, pt. 1, pp. 1–102. Reprint. Peking: Peking Natural History Bulletin, 1931.

Schurman, Franz, and Orville Schell. *The China Reader: Imperial China*. New York: Vintage, 1967.

Seagrave, Sterling. *The Soong Dynasty*. New York: Harper and Row, 1985.

Stalberg, Roberta Helmer, and Ruth Nesi. *China's Crafts*. New York: Eurasia Press, 1980.

Stuart, G. A. *Chinese Materia Medica—Vegetable Kingdom*. Shanghai: American Presbyterian Mission Press, 1928.

Tsai, Hung, and Wu Lien-Teh. *The Practice of Surgery and Anesthetics in Ancient China*. Proceedings of the First Pan-Pacific Surgical Conference, Honolulu, Hawaii, 1929.

Tung, Chi-Ming. *An Outline History of China*. Beijing: Foreign Language Press, 1958–1959. Reprint. Hong Kong: Joint Publishing Co., 1979.

Veith, Ilza. *The Yellow Emperor's Classic of Internal Medicine*. Berkeley and Los Angeles: University of California Press, 1966.

Waley, Arthur. *The Adventures of Monkey*. New York: John Day, 1943.

Wallnofer, Heinrich, and Anna Von Rottausher. *Chinese Folk Medicine*. New York: Crown, 1965.

Wang, Shao Chi. *China and Her Great Men*. Taiwan: Chinese Association For Advancement of Science, 1960.

Werner, E. T. C. *A Dictionary of Chinese Mythol-*

ogy. Shanghai: Kelly and Walsh, 1932. Reprint. New York: Julian Press, 1961.

————. *Myths and Legends of China*. London: Harrap, 1922.

Williams, C. A. S. *Outlines of Chinese Symbolism and Art Motives*. 3rd revised edition. Shanghai: Kelly and Walsh, 1941. Reprint. Tokyo: Charles E. Tuttle, 1976.

Williams, S. Wells. *The Middle Kingdom*. 2 vols. London: W. H. Allen, 1883.

Wong, K. Chimin, and Wu Lien-Teh. *History of Chinese Medicine*. 2nd ed. Shanghai: National Quarantine Service, 1936. Reprint. New York: AMS Press, 1973.

Wu, Luen Tak. *Magnificent China*. Hong Kong: Liang You Book Co., 1966.

Yang, Martin C. *A Chinese Village*. New York: Columbia University Press, 1945.

INDEX

ABOUT THE AUTHOR

K. S. Tom is an obstetrician and gynecologist who has devoted many years to studying the history and culture of China. He is a graduate of the University of Hawaii and received his M.D. from Stritch-Loyola University in Chicago. Dr. Tom was the first trained obstetrician and gynecologist to be certified to practice in Hawaii and has served as chief of obstetrics and gynecology at Kapiolani Maternity Hospital and St. Francis Hospital in Honolulu. He is currently clinical professor of obstetrics and gynecology at the John A. Burns School of Medicine, University of Hawaii.